Los Angeles

must SEES

Chief Editor   Cynthia Clayton Ochterbeck
Senior Editor   M. Linda Lee
Contributing Writers   Shea Dean, Irvina Lew, Megan Thompson
Production Coordinator Allison M. Simpson
Cartography   Peter Wrenn
Photo Editor   Brigitta L. House
Documentation   Doug Rogers
Production   Octavo Design and Production
                        Apopka, Florida
Cover Design   Paris Venise Design
                        Paris, 17e
Printing and Binding Quebecor World
                        Laval, Québec

Contact us:

Michelin North America
One Parkway South
Greenville, SC 29615
USA
800-423-0485
www.michelin-us.com
email: TheGreenGuide-us@us.michelin.com

Special Sales:

For information regarding bulk sales, customized editions and premium sales, please contact our Customer Service Departments:

USA – 800-423-0485   **Canada** – 800-361-8236

Manufacture française des pneumatiques Michelin
Société en commandite par actions au capital de 304 000 000 EUR
Place des Carmes-Déchaux – 63 Clermont-Ferrand (France)
R.C.S. Clermont-FD B 855 800 507

Note to the reader:

While every effort is made to ensure that all information in this guide is correct and up-to-date, Michelin Travel Publications (Michelin North America, Inc.) accepts no liability for any direct, indirect or consequential losses howsoever caused so far as such can be excluded by law.

Admission prices listed for sights in this guide are for a single adult, unless otherwise specified.

Welcome to Los Angeles

Table of Contents

Table of Contents

THE MICHELIN STARS

For more than 75 years, travelers have used the Michelin stars to take the guesswork out of planning a trip. Our star-rating system helps you make the best decision on where to go, what to do, and what to see. A three-star rating means it's one of the "absolutelys"; two stars means it's one of the "should sees"; and one star says it's one of the "sees" — a must if you have the time.

★★★ Absolutely Must See
★★ Really Must See
★ Must See

Three-Star Sights★★★

Disneyland Park★★★

Disneyland Resort★★★

The Getty Center★★★

Hollywood★★★

Huntington Library, Art Collections and Botanical Gardens★★★

Los Angeles County Museum of Art★★★

Mission Santa Barbara★★★

Norton Simon Museum★★★

Palm Springs Aerial Tramway★★★

Rodeo Drive★★★

Queen Mary★★★

Universal Studios Hollywood★★★

Walt Disney Concert Hall★★★

Two-Star Sights★★

Beverly Hills★★

Biltmore Hotel★★

Bradbury Building★★

Disney's California Adventure★★

Eastern Columbia Building★★

El Capitan Theatre★★

Exposition Park★★

Gamble House★★

Grauman's Chinese Theatre★★

Griffith Park★★

Hollyhock House★★

Hollywood Boulevard★★

Hollywood Bowl★★

Huntington Art Gallery★★

Joshua Tree National Park★★

Long Beach Aquarium of the Pacific★★

Los Angeles City Hall★★
Los Angeles Zoo and
  Botanical Garden★★
Mission San Juan
  Capistrano★★
Museum of Contemporary
  Art★★
Museum of the American
  West★★
Museum of Tolerance★★
Natural History Museum of
  Los Angeles County★★
Pacific Design Center★★
Page Museum at the La Brea
  Tar Pits ★★

Palm Springs★★
Palm Springs Desert
  Museum★★
Pasadena★★
Petersen Automotive
  Museum★★
Santa Barbara★★
Santa Barbara County
  Courthouse★★
Santa Monica Pier★★
Skirball Cultural Center★★
Southwest Museum★★
Sunset Strip★★
Venice Beach★★

One-Star Sights★

Avila Adobe★
Bergamot Station Arts
  Center★
Beverly Hills Hotel★
California Plaza★
California ScienCenter★
Catalina Island★
Crystal Cathedral★
Descanso Gardens★
Dorothy Chandler Pavilion★
Downtown★
Egyptian Theatre★
El Pueblo de Los Angeles
  Historic Monument★
Geffen Contemporary at
  MOCA★
Grand Central Market★
Hollywood and Highland★
Hollywood Entertainment
  Museum★
Hollywood Roosevelt Hotel★
Hollywood Sign★
James Irvine Garden★
Japanese American National
  Museum★
La Brea Tar Pits★
Laguna Art Museum★
Laguna Beach★
Library Tower★
Los Angeles Central Library★
Long Beach★
Lummis House★
Malibu★

Melrose Avenue★
Museum of Television
  & Radio★
Newport Beach★
Olvera Street★
Orange County Museum
  of Art★
Original Farmers Market★
Pantages Theatre★
Pershing Square★
Pico House★
Richard Nixon Library and
  Birthplace★
Rose Bowl★
San Gabriel Arcangel
  Mission★
Santa Barbara Museum of
  Art★
Santa Barbara Museum of
  Natural History★
Santa Monica★
Sunset Boulevard★★
Third Street Promenade★
Union Station★
Universal City Walk★
Venice★
Virginia Robinson Gardens★
Walk of Fame★
Warner Bros. Studios★
Westin Bonaventure Hotel★
Will Rogers State Historic
  Park★
Wiltern Theatre★

January

Golden Globe Awards 800-345-2210
Beverly Hills www.beverlyhillsbehere.com

Little Tokyo Welcomes the New Year 800-228-2452
January 1st, Downtown www.visitlanow.com

Pasadena Tournament of Roses Parade 626-449-4100
Colorado Blvd. to Orange Grove Blvd., Pasadena
www.tournamentofroses.com

Rose Bowl Game 626-449-4100
Rose Bowl Stadium, Pasadena
www.tournamentofroses.com

February

African American Heritage 213-623-4352, ext. 327
  Celebrations
Angelus Plaza www.visitlanow.com

March

Academy Awards 800-228-2452
Hollywood www.visitlanow.com

LA Marathon/Acura Bike 310-444-5544
Downtown www.visitlanow.com

West Week Design 310-360-6419
West Hollywood www.pacificdesigncenter.org

April

Blessing of the Animals 213-625-5045
El Pueblo de Los Angeles,
  Downtown www.olvera-street.com/fiestas.htm

May

Annual Art & Design Walk 323-289-2525
West Hollywood www.visitwesthollywood.com

Annual Venice Garden Tour 310-390-6641
Venice www.venicegardentour.org.

Cinco de Mayo Celebration 213-625-5045
El Pueblo de Los Angeles,
  Downtown www.olvera-street.com/fiestas.htm

Old Pasadena Summer Fest 626-797-6803
Memorial Day, Central Park in
  Old Pasadena www.oldpasadenasummerfest.com

Santa Monica Festival 310-458-8350
Clover Park www.arts.santa-monica.org

June

Annual in the Water Boat Show 310-645-5151
Marina del Rey www.mdrboatshow.com

Art & Design Walk 310-289-2525
West Hollywood www.visitwesthollywood.com

Christopher Street West/LA Pride 800-368-6020
West Hollywood www.lapride.org

Twilight Dance Series 310-458-8901
Summer Saturdays on
 Santa Monica Pier www.twilightdance.org

July

Concourse on Rodeo 800-345-2210
Rodeo Drive,
 Beverly Hills www.beverlyhillsbehere.com

Old Pasadena Jazzfest 818-771-5544
Central Park in Old Pasadena www.omegaevents.com

August

Santa Monica Drive-In Movie Series 310-264-4274
Tuesdays at 6:30pm, Santa Monica Pier www.smff.com

September

City of Los Angeles Triathlon 714-978-1528
Venice Beach www.latriathlon.com

Tribute To Style 800-345-2210
Rodeo Drive,
 Beverly Hills www.beverlyhillsbehere.com

October

Craftsman Weekend 626-441-6333
Pasadena www.pasadenaheritage.org

Flower and Garden Show 800-345-2210
Greystone Mansion,
 Beverly Hills www.beverlyhillsbehere.com

Halloween Costume Carnaval 800-368-6020
West Hollywood www.visitwesthollywood.com

November

American Film Market 310-446-1000
Santa Monica www.afma.com

Doo Dah Parade 626-440-7379
Pasadena www.pasadenadoodahparade.com

Holiday Lighting Ceremony 800-345-2210
Beverly Hills www.beverlyhillsbehere.com

December

Las Posadas 213-625-5045
El Pueblo de Los Angeles,
 Downtown www.olvera-street.com/fiestas.htm

Marina del Rey Annual 310-822-9455
 Holiday Boat Parade
Fisherman's Wharf, Marina del Rey www.mdrlights.org

Area Codes

To call between area codes in the LA area, dial 1 + area code + seven-digit number.

Downtown Los Angeles: **213**

Beverly Hills, coastal communities: **310**

Hollywood and West Hollywood: **323**

Long Beach: **562**

Pasadena: **646**

Studio City, Burbank and Ventura: **818**

Web Sites

Here are some additional web sites to help you plan your trip:

www.allaroundlosangeles.com

www.downtownla.com

www.experiencela.com

www.seeing-stars.com

www.dot.ca.gov

www.losangelesalmanac.com

PLANNING YOUR TRIP

Before you go, contact the following agencies to obtain maps and information about sightseeing, accommodations, travel packages, recreational opportunities and special events.

Los Angeles Convention & Visitors Bureau

333 S. Hope St., Los Angeles, CA 90071
213-236-2300 or 800-228-2452; www.lacvb.com or www.visitlanow.com

Beverly Hills Convention & Visitors Bureau

239 S. Beverly Dr., Beverly Hills, CA 90210
310-285-2438 or 800-345-2210; www.beverlyhillscvb.com

Hollywood Visitor Information Center

6541 Hollywood Blvd.
213-461-4213; www.hollywoodcoc.org

Long Beach Area Convention & Visitors Bureau

One World Trade Center, Long Beach, CA 90831
562-495-8350 or 800-452-7829; www.visitlongbeach.com

Santa Monica Convention & Visitors Bureau

203 Santa Monica Place, Santa Monica, CA 90401
310-393-7593 or 800-544-5319; www.santamonica.com

Pasadena Convention & Visitors Bureau

171 S. Los Robles Ave., Pasadena, CA 91101
626-795-9311 or 800-307-7977; www.pasadenacal.com

West Hollywood Convention & Visitors Bureau

8687 Melrose Ave., West Hollywood, CA 90069
310-289-2525 or 800-368-6020; www.visitwesthollywood.com

In the News

The city's main daily newspaper is the *Los Angeles Times* (*www.latimes.com*). You'll find weekly entertainment listings in its Thursday *Calendar* section and in LA's weekly free newspaper, *LA Weekly* (*www.laweekly.com*). Other area newspapers and publications include the *Los Angeles Magazine* (*www.lamag.com*) and *LA Downtown News* (*www.ladowntownnews.com*).

Visitor Centers

Downtown Los Angeles Visitor Information Center

685 Figueroa St., between Wilshire Blvd. & 7th St.
213-689-8822
Open year-round Mon–Fri 8am–5pm, Sat 8:30am–5pm

CityPass – Consider buying a CityPass booklet for substantially discounted admission to many LA and Southern California attractions. A **Hollywood City-Pass** *($69 adults; $49 ages 3–9; good for 30 days after first use)* gets you into five famous Hollywood attractions: Universal Studios, Kodak Theatre (guided tour), the Hollywood Entertainment Museum, Starline Tours of Hollywood, and the Museum of the American West.

If you plan to head outside of the LA area, the **Southern California CityPass** *($172 adults; $129 ages 3–9; good for two weeks after first use)* includes a 3-day Disneyland *Park Hopper Ticket,* as well as admission to Knott's Theme Park (in Buena Park), and 1-day passes to Sea World (San Diego) and the San Diego Zoo.

TIPS FOR SPECIAL VISITORS

Disabled Travelers – Federal law requires that businesses (including hotels and restaurants) provide access for the disabled, devices for the hearing impaired, and designated parking spaces. For further information, contact the Society for Accessible Travel and Hospitality (SATH), 347 Fifth Ave., Suite 610, New York, NY 10016 *(212-447-7284; www.sath.org)*.

All national parks have facilities for the disabled, and offer free or discounted passes. For details, contact the National Park Service *(Office of Public Inquiries, P.O. Box 37127, Room 1013, Washington, DC 20013-7127; 202-208-4747; www.nps.gov)*.

Passengers who will need assistance with train or bus travel should give advance notice to Amtrak *(800-872-7245 or 800-523-6590/TDD; www.amtrak.com)* or Greyhound *(800-752-4841 or 800-345-3109/TDD; www.greyhound.com)*. Make reservations for hand-controlled cars in advance with the rental company.

Local Lowdown – The following publications provide detailed information about access for the disabled in the Los Angeles area:

- **LAX** offers the *Guidebook for Disabled People* to help the disabled get in LA *(to order a copy, call 310-646-5260)*.
- **Los Angeles Metropolitan Transit Authority** *(800-266-6883; www.mta.net)* offers reduced fares for disabled passengers.
- **Los Angeles Commission on Disabilities** *(213-974-1053 or 213-974-1707/TDD)* can help you find resources and information about traveling in LA with disabilities.

Senior Citizens – Many hotels, attractions and restaurants offer discounts to visitors age 62 or older (proof of age may be required). The **American Association of Retired Persons** (AARP), *(601 E St. NW, Washington, DC 20049; 202-424-3410; www.aarp.com)* offers discounts to its members.

Important Numbers	
Emergency (police/fire/ambulance, 24hrs)	911
Police (non-emergency)	877-275-5273
Medical Services	
House Calls USA	800-468-3537
Dental Emergencies (24hrs)	
UCLA College of Dentistry	310-825-2337
24-hour Pharmacies:	
Rite Aid (4 locations):	
334 S. Vermont Ave., at Third St.	213-381-5257
1637 N. Vermont Ave., at Hollywood Blvd.	323-664-9854
7900 W. Sunset Blvd., West Hollywood	323-876-4466
300 N. Cannon Dr., Beverly Hills	310-273-3561
Time	310-976-1616
Weather	310-976-1212

WHEN TO GO

Temperate weather is one of the most constant pleasures in LA. The climate is dependably sunny and mild, and even in December and January, the beaches are crowded with walkers, joggers and in-line skaters. Although it rarely rains, January and February are the wettest months. Remember, LA is basically a desert, so bring a light jacket for early morning and evening. Spring and summer are peak tourist seasons; if you visit during those times, expect large crowds at all the major attractions. If your heart is set on being in the studio audience for a particular TV show, consider visiting in the off-season.

> **Smog Alert**
>
> If you suffer from any chronic breathing conditions or respiratory health problems, you should avoid LA in the summer, when smog levels are at their highest and air quality is at its worst.

Seasonal Temperatures in LA *(recorded at LAX)*

	Jan	Apr	July	Oct
Avg. High	66°F/19°C	67°F/20°C	75°F/24°C	74°F/24°C
Avg. Low	48°F/9°C	53°F/12°C	63°F/17°C	59°F/15°C

GETTING THERE

By Air – Los Angeles is served by several airports, three of which are in LA County. As many domestic travelers have discovered, it is often more convenient (and less expensive) to fly into one of the smaller airports.

Los Angeles International Airport (LAX) – 17mi southwest of downtown LA, on W. Century Blvd. at S. Sepulveda Blvd. *(310-646-5252; www.lawa.org)*.

Burbank Airport (BUR) – 13mi northwest of downtown LA, on Thornton Ave. at N. Hollywood Way *(818-840-8840; www.burbankairport.com)*.

Long Beach Airport (LGB) – 22mi southwest of downtown LA via I-405 to Lakewood Blvd. *(562-570-2600; www.lgb.org)*.

John Wayne Airport (SNA) – 36mi southeast of downtown LA via I-405 to Airport Way *(949-252-5200; www.ocair.com)*.

Ontario International Airport (ONT) – 35mi east of downtown LA via I-10 to Grove Ave. *(909-937-2700; www.lawa.org)*.

By Train – You can reach Los Angeles by means of five train lines, all run by Amtrak *(800-872-7245; www.amtrak.com)*. Historic **Union Station★** *(800 N. Alameda St.)* is LA's rail hub, serving as the stop for all five train lines and providing connections to the Metro Link subway, the Metro Rail commuter line, several bus lines and to DASH *(see p 14)*.

By Bus – Greyhound serves LA's main bus terminal, located at 1715 N. Cahuenga Blvd. *(for fares, schedules & routes, call 800-229-9424 or visit www.greyhound.com)*.

By Car – Los Angeles has ready access to I-5, which runs from Canada to Mexico. I-10 enters the city from the southeast; I-15 connects directly to San Diego and, farther on, to Las Vegas.

Car Rental Companies

Car Rental Company	Reservations	Internet
Alamo	800-462-5266	www.alamo.com
Avis	800-230-4898	www.avis.com
Budget	800-527-0700	www.drivebudget.com
Dollar	800-800-4000	www.dollar.com
Enterprise	800-736-8222	www.enterprise.com
Hertz	800-654-3131	www.hertz.com
National	800-227-7368	www.nationalcar.com
Thrifty	800-847-4389	www.thrifty.com

GETTING AROUND

By Car – The city Dionne Warwick referred to in song as "a great big highway" is indeed a driver's town, and its vehicles rack up more than 90 million miles daily. The roads, sprawling out over 467sq mi in the city and 4,081sq mi in the county, can remain clogged throughout the day. Even so, it's not unusual to see drivers hurling down the interstates at rates far exceeding the speed limit.

Valet Parking – There's no need to spend hours searching for a parking spot in LA. Here, two magic words take the problem out of your hands: valet parking. From hotels and restaurants to theaters and doctor's offices, most businesses offer this service, which will cost you $3.50–$4.50 plus a $1 tip. Parking garages are available but tend to be expensive (some cost $2 for 20 minutes). Metered parking is scarce and time limits are strictly enforced.

Must Know: Practical Information

LA Freeways

Although there are 528mi of freeway and 382mi of highway in and around LA, the following connect most major tourist destinations. Keep in mind that I-405 is the major north/south artery, and I-10 is the major east/west thoroughfare. Take US-101 Downtown and to the San Fernando Valley; Route 110 to Pasadena; and I-5 to Anaheim and Orange County.

Number	Name
Rte. 2	Glendale Freeway
I-5	Golden State Freeway (north of Downtown)
	Santa Ana Freeway (south of Downtown)
I-10	Santa Monica Freeway (west of Downtown)
	San Bernardino Freeway (east of Downtown)
Rte. 14	Antelope Valley Freeway
Rte. 22	Garden Grove Freeway
Rte. 57	Orange Freeway
Rte. 60	Pomona Freeway
Rte. 90	Marina Freeway
Rte. 91	Artesia Freeway-Gardena Freeway
US-101 (south of Rte. 134) & Rte. 170	Hollywood Freeway (north of Downtown)
US-101 (west of Rte. 170) & Rte. 134	Ventura Freeway
I-105	Glen Anderson Freeway
Rte. 110	Pasadena Freeway
I-110	Harbor Freeway
Rte. 118	Ronald Reagan Freeway
I-210	Foothill Freeway
I-405	San Diego Freeway
I-605	San Gabriel River Freeway
I-710	Long Beach Freeway

By Foot – Although it's said that nobody walks in LA, it is possible to get around without a car. If you stay at a centrally located hotel downtown, in Beverly Hills, West Hollywood, Hollywood or Santa Monica, for example, you'll be near shops, cinemas, attractions and restaurants.

Public Transportation

The **Metropolitan Transit Authority** (MTA) coordinates the trains, commuter lines, subways and buses in Los Angeles. Its 1,433sq mi service area is available to more than 9.6 million people. With its 200 bus lines, MTA is a reliable and inexpensive way to tour Los Angeles. For schedules, routes and fares, call or check online: *213-266-2883 or 800-266-6883; www.mta.net*.

Bus and Light Rail – MTA also manages LA's rail networks. **Metrolink,** a system of high-speed commuter trains, connects Los Angeles with outlying communities in the LA area *(800-371-5465; www.metrolinktrains.com; operates daily 5am–11pm; $1.25 one-way, 25¢ transfers)*.

Los Angeles Department of Transportation (LADOT) operates a number of shuttle buses in Los Angeles County *(213-580-1177 or 213-580-1188/TDD; www.lacity.org/ladot)*. The most notable of these, **DASH**, covers several neighborhoods including Downtown and Hollywood.

Subway – LA's subway system, **MetroRail**, is also operated by MTA. Based in Union Station *(800 N. Alameda St.)*, the four subway lines can make travel quick and inexpensive. Each line is designated by color. The **Blue Line** travels to Long Beach; the **Red Line** goes to North Hollywood. Take the **Green Line** to and from Los Angeles International Airport (LAX), or the **Gold Line** out to Pasadena.

By Taxi – *www.taxicabsla.org.* Only cabs bearing the City of Los Angeles Taxicab Seal are authorized to operate within Los Angeles. There is a $38 flat fare for traveling between LAX and downtown. For all other rides, rates are $2 for the first 1/10mi or 32 seconds and 20¢ for each additional 1/10mi or 32 seconds waiting in traffic. If you are departing from LAX and heading to a neighborhood other than downtown, you'll pay a $2.50 surcharge. Try to find cabs based in your destination neighborhood unless you know the area well. It's often faster to call for a cab, rather than attempt to hail one from the street.

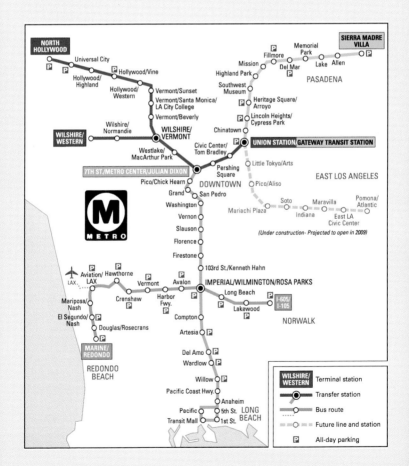

Must Know: Practical Information

FOREIGN VISITORS

Visitors from outside the US can obtain information from the Los Angeles Convention and Visitors Bureau *(213-236-2300; www.lacvb.com)* or from the US embassy or consulate in their country of residence. For a complete list of American consulates and embassies abroad, visit the US State Department Bureau of Consular Affairs listing on the Internet at: *http://travel.state.gov/links.html.*

Entry Requirements – Travelers entering the United States under the Visa Waiver Program (VWP) must have a machine-readable passport. Any traveler without a machine-readable passport will be required to obtain a visa before entering the US. Citizens of VWP countries are permitted to enter the US for general business or tourist purposes for a maximum of 90 days without needing a visa. Requirements for the Visa Waiver Program can be found at the Department of State's Visa Services Web site *(http://travel.state.gov/vwp.html).*

All citizens of non-participating countries must have a visitor's visa. Upon entry, nonresident foreign visitors must present a valid passport and a round-trip transportation ticket. Canadian citizens are not required to present a passport or visa, but they must present a valid picture ID and proof of citizenship. Naturalized Canadian citizens should carry their citizenship papers.

US Customs – All articles brought into the US must be declared at the time of entry. Prohibited items: plant material; firearms and ammunition (if not for sporting purposes); meat or poultry products. For information, contact the US Customs Service, 1300 Pennsylvania Ave. NW, Washington, DC 20229 *(202-354-1000; www.cbp.gov).*

Money and Currency Exchange – Visitors can exchange currency at local banks in the business district downtown as well as in the international terminal at LAX. Banks, stores, restaurants and hotels accept traveler's checks with a picture ID. To report a lost or stolen credit card: **American Express** *(800-528-4800);* **Diners Club** *(800-234-6377);* **MasterCard** *(800-307-7309);* **Visa** *(800-336-8472).*

Driving in the US – Visitors bearing valid driver's licenses issued by their country of residence are not required to obtain an International Driver's License. Drivers must carry vehicle registration and/or rental contract, and proof of automobile insurance at all times. Gasoline is sold by the gallon (1 gal=3.8 liters). Vehicles in the US are driven on the right-hand side of the road.

Electricity – Voltage in the US is 120 volts AC, 60 Hz. Foreign-made appliances may need AC adapters (available at specialty travel and electronics stores) and North American flat-blade plugs.

Taxes and Tipping – Prices displayed in the US do not include the California sales tax of 8.5%, which is not reimbursable. It is customary to give a small gift of money—a tip—for services rendered, to waiters (15–20% of bill), porters ($1 per bag), chamber maids ($1 per day), valet parkers ($1) and cab drivers (15% of fare). If your hotel concierge has provided exceptional service, $5 is a standard tip.

Time Zone – Los Angeles is in the Pacific Standard Time (PST) zone, eight hours behind Greenwich Mean Time, and three hours behind New York City.

Measurement Equivalents

Degrees Fahrenheit	95°	86°	77°	68°	59°	50°	41°	32°	23°	14°
Degrees Celsius	35°	30°	25°	20°	15°	10°	5°	0°	-5°	-10°

1 inch = 2.5 centimeters   1 foot = 30.48 centimeters   1 mile = 1.6 kilometers
1 pound = 0.45 kilograms   1 quart = 0.9 liters   1 gallon = 3.78 liters

ACCOMMODATIONS

For a list of suggested accommodations, see Must Stay.

Hotel Reservation Services:

Central Reservation Services – 800-555-7555; www.reservation-services.com.
City Hotel Finder – 888-649-6331; www.cityhotelfinder.com.
Express Hotel Reservations – 800-407-3351; www.express-res.com.

Hostels – *www.hostels.com.* A no-frills, inexpensive alternative to hotels, hostels are a great choice for budget travelers. Prices average $25–$75 per night.
Venice Beach Cotel – 25 Windward Ave., Venice Beach; 310-399-7649;
www.venicebeachcotel.com.
Orbit Hotel and Hostel – 7950 Melrose Ave., West Hollywood; 323-655-1510;
www.orbithotel.com.
USA Hostels Hollywood – 1624 Schrader Blvd., Hollywood; 323-462-3777;
www.usahostels.com/hollywood.

SPORTS

Angelenos love their sports. Los Angeles' professional sports teams include:

Sport/Team	Season	Venue	Phone	Web site
Baseball (NL) LA Dodgers	Apr–Oct	Dodger Stadium	800-636-3437	www.losangeles.dodgers.mlb.com.
Baseball (AL) Anaheim Angels	Apr–Oct	Angel Stadium	888-796-4256	www.anaheim.angels.mlb.com
Basketball (NBA) LA Lakers	Nov–Apr	Staples Center	213-480-3232	www.nba.com/lakers
Basketball (NBA) LA Clippers	Nov–Apr	Staples Center	213-742-7555	www.nba.com/clippers
Basketball (WNBA) LA Sparks	May–Aug	Staples Center	310-426-6033	www.wnba.com/sparks
Hockey (NHL) LA Kings	Oct–Apr	Staples Center	213-742-7100	www.lakings.com
Hockey (NHL) Anaheim Mighty Ducks	Oct–Apr	Arrowhead Pond	877-945-3946	www.mightyducks.com
Soccer (MLS) LA Galaxy	Apr–Oct	Home Depot Center	310-630-2200	www.lagalaxy.com

Los Angeles

City of Angels: Los Angeles

Tinsel Town, La-La Land, Planet Hollywood—speak of any of these and you speak of Los Angeles, the largest metropolis in the nation. The sprawling, throbbing melting pot that is the LA metropolitan area occupies some 5,000 square miles and encompasses 88 separate cities. Its residents know an economic and cultural diversity that seems at first schizophrenic, yet they all share a love of their mythic city. Call it what you will, Los Angeles is home.

LA wasn't always the dynamic place you see today. Long before the Spanish arrived, the land now covered by Los Angeles was a peaceful, albeit dry and dusty, hunting and fishing ground for the Chumash and other tribes. The first Spanish explorer to see the shoreline here was Juan Cabrillo, who in 1542 sailed up the coast to Santa Barbara. But colonization didn't begin in earnest until more than two hundred years later.

In 1781 the Spanish governor of California, Felipe de Neve, called for volunteers to settle a new town on the Porciúncula River; the hearty group of 44 *pobladores* (settlers) who answered Neve's call established **El Pueblo de Los Angeles**. The town continued under Spanish rule until Mexico won its independence from Spain in 1821. In the decades that followed, Mexican governors promoted the colonization of Alta California by granting huge parcels of land to loyal subjects and ambitious foreigners. By the time it was designated capital of Mexican California in 1845, the fledgling city of Los Angeles had become the commercial and social center for a region of vast cattle ranches and vineyards operated by a handful of wealthy families.

The *rancheros'* bubble burst in the 1860s, however, as questions about the legality of their land grants coupled with a three-year drought pushed many ranch owners into bankruptcy. Their lands eventually passed into American hands.

Buoyed by the burgeoning citrus industry and the discovery of oil in the area, LA's economy prospered at the beginning of the 20C. Despite this new wealth, the city's growth was severely limited by lack of water. Enter engineer William Mulholland, who initiated a

> ### A Chain of Missions
>
> In 1767 the King of Spain turned to the Franciscan Order to extend Spanish control northward into Alta California. Father **Junipero Serra** (1713–1784) was named as the leader of the Sacred Expedition that left Baja California for San Diego in 1769. Over the next 54 years, 20 missions were established in a chain that stretched from San Diego north to San Francisco. Located a day's travel apart, the missions were linked by a trail known as **El Camino Real**, the Royal Highway—a route traced today by Highway 101.

$24.5 million project to bring water to the city from the Owens Valley 250mi north. Officially opened in 1913, the **Los Angeles Aqueduct** enabled the city to expand its boundaries; by the 1920s, LA had incorporated the neighboring communities of Beverly Hills, Santa Monica, Long Beach and Pasadena.

The first decade of the 20C brought the infant motion-picture industry from New York City and Chicago to the LA area, whose mild climate was conducive to year-round outdoor filming. Centered in Hollywood, the city's film industry was producing 80 percent of the world's feature films by 1920. Movie stars snapped up valuable property in the Hollywood hills and in nearby Beverly Hills, infusing these communities with the glittering aura of the movies. Downtown, extravagant Art Deco landmarks sprang up, along with grand hotels.

Development in the South Bay area exploded after World War II. As the freeway system connected the branching communities, Los Angeles, long dependent on the automobile, spread north, south, west, and east to the San Fernando Valley. In the 21C, this mammoth city faces the challenges of any major metropolis—economic recession, racial unrest, environmental concerns—in addition to the natural disasters, such as fires, mudslides and earthquakes, dictated by the area's climate and geography.

Today LA's diverse population still speaks in many different accents. They came here for different reasons: for economic advancement, to follow a dream, for freedom, or for the sunny Southern California climate. But whether they hail from the East Coast or the Middle East, the Midwest or Mexico, Angelenos speak one language when it comes to their beloved city. They know that the sense of possibility is strong here. Indeed, the sky's the limit in the City of Angels.

Fast Facts for Los Angeles
• **Population:** 3.8 million (City of LA); 9.5 million (LA County)
• **Size:** City of Los Angeles encompasses 467 square miles, plus 76 miles of coast-line in the Metropolitan Area.
• **Number of Stars on the Walk of Fame:** 2,221—and counting
• **Number of Commuters:** More than 23 million car trips are made in a 24-hour period on any given weekday in LA.
• **Number of Certified Plastic Surgeons in LA County:** 200 (now, *that's* a lot of face lifts!).

Los Angeles is home to such a diverse group of neighborhoods that a drive across town can seem like a dizzying world tour. Unlike cities such as New York and San Francisco, many of LA's "neighborhoods" are actually separate incorporated cities. Each one has something unique to offer, though, and it's worth spending some time to soak in their ambience. Here's a sampling of the city's melting pot.

Hollywood★★★

Roughly bounded by Franklin, La Brea, Melrose & Western Aves. Visitor information: 7018 Hollywood Blvd., 323-469-8311; www.hollywoodcoc.org.

It's been a while since Hollywood was the true center of the motion-picture industry—most of the neighborhood's big studios have found more spacious (and less expensive) digs in Burbank and environs. But for the starry-eyed and the cinephilic, Hollywood offers plenty to see and do.

"Hollywoodland," as it was originally called, was founded in 1883 by Kansas prohibitionist H.H. Wilcox. It was annexed to LA in 1910. The movie biz soon followed. After the first studio opened here in 1911, five East Coast companies followed suit, drawn by the scenery and the year-round sunshine, ideal for outdoor film shoots. The golden age of Hollywood film—the 1930s and 1940s—corresponded to the golden age of the neighborhood itself. After several decades of neglect, a recent 30-year, billion-dollar facelift has readied the neighborhood once again for its close-up.

Universal Studios Hollywood ★★★ – *100 Universal City Plaza. See Studios.*

Hollywood Boulevard★★
Between Gower & Sycamore Sts.

Some of old Hollywood's grandest movie palaces stand along this famous stretch. Stop for a moment at the intersection of **Hollywood and Vine** and try to imagine all your favorite Hollywood stars of the 1930s and 1940s. Chances are they once stood right where you are, on their way to or from Sardi's and the Brown Derby, the era's most renowned hangouts (now both closed).

The Hollywood Roosevelt Hotel★

7000 Hollywood Blvd. 323-769-7260 or 800-950-7667. www.hollywoodroosevelt.com.

Known as "the Home of the Stars," the Spanish Colonial landmark has welcomed a who's-who roster of guests throughout the years, including Louis B. Mayer, Douglas Fairbanks, Mary Pickford and Marilyn Monroe. The first Oscars ceremony took place here in the Blossom Room in 1929. Today **Feinstein's at the Cinegrill** showcases top-notch entertainment.

El Capitan Theatre★★ – *6838 Hollywood Blvd. 800-347-6396. disney.go.com/disneypictures/el_capitan.*

Though its over-the-top decor suggests Tinseltown touches, the Spanish Colonial theater (1926) was actually "Hollywood's first home of spoken drama"—that is, "legitimate" theater—not movies. That didn't last, though. In 1941 the silver screen was installed for the world premiere of Orson Welles' *Citizen Kane*. Today it's the highest-grossing single-screen theater in the country. The East India-style interior, which cost $1.2 million to complete, sparkles with ornate grillwork and gold leaf.

Grauman's Chinese Theatre★★ – *6925 Hollywood Blvd. 323-464-8111. www.mann.moviefone.com.* This fantastic 1927 movie palace, named for its previous owner, Sid Grauman, is one of the most recognizable cinemas in the world. The monumental exterior is dominated by a mansard-roofed pagoda topped with stylized flames and flanked with white-marble dogs.

• **Forecourt**★★ – "For Mr. Grauman. All Happiness. Judy Garland." That's just one of the notes you'll see in the multicolored cement here, along with the hand- and footprints of 200-plus Hollywood stars. Some luminaries went a bit further: Betty Grable gave us casts of her shapely legs; Gene Autry, the hoofprints of his horse; Bob Hope and Jimmy Durante, nose prints.

Egyptian Theatre★ – **[B]** *refers to map on inside back cover. 6712 Hollywood Blvd. 323-466-3456. www.americancinematheque.com. Tours Tue—Sun 10:30am—4pm. $7.* Showman Sid Grauman built this Egyptian-inspired wonder in 1922 in honor of the discovery of King Tut's tomb. Now beautifully restored, the theater screens the documentary *Forever Hollywood* on weekends.

Hollywood & Highland★ – **[A]** *refers to map on inside back cover. 6801 Hollywood Blvd. 323-467-6412. www.hollywoodandhighland.com. Open year-round Mon—Sat 10am—10pm, Sun 10am—7pm.* Looming large over Grauman's

Chinese Theater, the signature project of Hollywood's revitalization is a $615 million shopping and entertainment center, with 70 retailers, 17 eateries, 6 movie screens, 2 nightclubs, and one hotel (the 640-room Renaissance Hollywood). You'll also find the **Kodak Theatre,** the new home of the Academy Awards *(see Performing Arts).*

Inside Historic Hollywood

To ogle the interiors of Disney's El Capitan Theatre, Grauman's Egyptian Theatre, the Blossom Room (home of the first Academy Awards ceremony), and a real Hollywood speakeasy, take a behind-the-scenes walking tour with **Red Line Tours** *(6773 Hollywood Blvd.; 323-402-1074; www.redlinetours.com; $20; reservations suggested).* To see the inside of Grauman's Chinese Theatre, catch a flick.

Hollywood Entertainment Museum★ – *7021 Hollywood Blvd. 323-465-7900. www.hollywoodmuseum.com Open Memorial Day–Labor Day Thu–Tue 10am–6pm; rest of the year 11am–6pm. Closed major holidays. $8.75.* See all the

magic of Hollywood, from special effects to makeup to set design, at this glittering interactive museum. Tour the original sets of *Star Trek, Cheers* and *The X-Files.* View caricatures of patrons of the famous Brown Derby restaurant. Learn about film noir and blaxploitation film. Or trip out on a recent display of psychedelic album covers (the museum embraces the music industry too).

Pantages Theatre★ *6233 Hollywood Blvd. 323-468-1770. www.nederlander.com/wc.* The concrete and black marble exterior is relatively understated compared to the interior, with its extravagantly detailed lobby and 2,812-seat auditorium. Long-running Broadway musicals are staged here. *See Performing Arts.*

Walk of Fame★ – *Both sides of Hollywood Blvd. from La Brea Ave. to Gower St.; both sides of Vine St. between Yucca & Sunset Blvd.* Envisioned in 1958 as a tribute to Hollywood's entertainment icons, the Walk of Fame has become one of Los Angeles' most visited landmarks. Between 1960 and 1961, the first 1,558 bronze stars were laid in the pink terrazzo sidewalk. Stars dedicated in 1994 pushed the total over 2,000. Most recently, actress Drew Barrymore, singer Celine Dion and cartoonist Dr. Seuss took their place in the pavement.

Barnsdall Art Park and Hollyhock House★★ – *4800 Hollywood Blvd. See Historic Sites.*

Hollywood Bowl★★ – *2301 N. Highland Ave. See Performing Arts.*

Hollywood Sign★ – *Griffith Park. See Landmarks.*

Scenic Drives

Stretching some 20mi from El Pueblo (Olvera Street) to the Pacific Ocean, **Sunset Boulevard**★ cuts through a dramatic cross section of life in Los Angeles. The street's most famous stretch is the 1.5mi **Sunset Strip**★★, a formerly unincorporated swath of land now home to the bars and clubs of increasingly trendy West Hollywood *(see Nightlife).* **Mulholland Drive**★, one of LA's most spectacular roads, follows a series of sinuous curves along the crest of the Santa Monica Mountains. The drive starts less than 1mi north of Hollywood Bowl *(at Cahuenga Blvd.)* and continues westward for 20mi to Calabasas.

Beverly Hills★★

Surrounded by Los Angeles on three sides and by West Hollywood on the fourth. Visitor information: 239 S. Beverly Dr. 310-248-1015 or 800-345-2210. www.beverlyhills.org or www.beverlyhillsbehere.com. Open Mon–Fri 8:30am–5pm.

Beverly Hills' gracious, impeccable residential streets ooze elegance; its posh restaurants and boutiques, casual chic. Dark sunglasses and high heels and floppy sun hats (who's *under* there?) abound, as do flashy cars, palm trees, manicured lawns, and toy poodles.

It didn't start this way. Beverly Hills was originally part of a Spanish land grant named El Rancho Rodeo de las Aguas. During the 19C it was mostly farmland, then, near the turn of the 20C, oil prospectors arrived, drilling 30 wells in El Rancho Rodeo.

Residential development started in earnest after the Beverly Hills Hotel was completed in 1912. Today the city ranks among the most moneyed enclaves in the country, and fully 91 percent of its 34,000 residents are white. The city is renowned for its luxury shopping and California cuisine, particularly in the so-called **Golden Triangle** bordered by Wilshire and Santa Monica boulevards and Cañon Drive. You can also get a good taste of the city by simply driving a

few of its most scenic streets, including **Sunset Boulevard**★, **Summit Drive**★, **Beverly Drive**, **Coldwater Canyon Drive**, and **Whittier Drive**, where the jacaranda trees burst forth with striking blue blossoms in the spring.

Rodeo Drive★★★ –
The ne-plus-ultra shopping experience. *See Must Shop.*

Beverly Hills Trolley

Departs from the corner of Rodeo Dr. & Dayton Way. 310-285-2438. www.beverlyhills.org. Tours July–Labor Day Tue–Sat noon-5pm; late Nov–Dec noon–4pm. Rest of year Sat only noon–4pm. No tours Dec 25. $5. If you don't want to drive through the city, and you're too tired to walk, hop on the old-fashioned-looking trolley for a relaxing, 40-minute docent-led "sights and scenes" tour, which takes you past the best of Beverly Hills' neighborhoods and attractions. If you're visiting LA between May and December, you may also want to check out the "art and architecture" tour *(Sat at 11am).*

Beverly Hills Hotel★

9641 Sunset Blvd. 310-276-2251. www.thebeverlyhillshotel.com.

The pink-stucco, Mission-style main building (1912) and its 21 secluded bungalows are partly concealed by 12 acres of lush tropical gardens, bestowing an air of privacy on its usually A-list guests. Charlie Chaplin, Marilyn Monroe and Marlene Dietrich all holed up here at one point or another. Howard Hughes rented bungalow No. 3 for years at a time. *See Must Stay.*

Polo Lounge

At the Beverly Hills Hotel. Movers and shakers repair to the secluded (but not too secluded) booths at this elegant rose-and-green lounge to network, strategize and pick at their wildly overpriced French toast. It's a fun scene. Be sure to bring your cell phone.

Museum of Television & Radio★ – *465 N. Beverly Dr. See Museums.*

Virginia Robinson Gardens★– *See Parks and Gardens.*

Beverly Hills Civic Center

455 N. Rexford Dr. 310-285-1000. www.beverlyhills.org. Open year-round Mon–Thu 7:30am–5:30pm; Fri 8am–5pm.

An elegant, Spanish Baroque-style tower crowned with a tiled dome, the City Hall (1932) sets the tone for a harmonious two-square-block contemporary addition, which links it to the public library *(no. 444)* and to the fire *(no. 445)* and police departments *(no. 464)* via elliptical courtyards.

Greystone Park

905 Loma Vista Dr. at Doheny Rd. 310-550-4796. Open May–Oct daily 10am–6pm. Rest of the year 10am–5pm.

The highlight of this 18.5-acre park is the 55-room English Tudor **Doheny Mansion**, built in 1928 by Edward (Charles) Doheny, Beverly Hills' first oil millionaire. Doheny spent about $4 million to construct the castle for his son, Ned (who was later murdered in it). Although the public can tour the mansion only during special events such as occasional high teas and theater performances, summer concerts and the November flower show *(visit www.beverlyhills.org for schedule)*, the former estate is still worth a look. A terraced hill featuring Italianate formal gardens slopes down toward Sunset Boulevard, offering remarkable views of downtown Los Angeles.

Pasadena★★

Visitor information: 171 S. Los Robles Ave.; 626-795-9311 or 800-307-7977; www.pasadenacal.com. Open Mon–Fri 8am–5pm, Sat 10am–4pm.

Located less than 9mi from downtown Los Angeles, Pasadena seems a world away from the bustle and sprawl of its urban neighbor. Bordered to the west by the Arroyo Seco ("dry gulch") of the San Gabriel Mountains, Pasadena moves at a leisurely pace and offers architecture and attractions worthy of a much larger city.

The name Pasadena comes from an Indian word meaning "crown of the valley." Development began in 1874, when a small group of Indiana farmers tried, unsuccessfully, to grow oranges here. Soon the town got hooked up to the railroad, bringing trainloads of rich sun-seekers from the Midwest and East Coast. Many of their lavish mansions survive today.

In 1899 Pasadena's elite Valley Hunt Club voted to mark New Year's Day with an annual parade of flower-decked coaches. Over the years, the carriages evolved into elaborate floats covered with roses. Today the **Tournament of Roses Parade** is a New Year's Day fixture both here and on televisions across the country. Every four years it is followed by the Rose Bowl college-football championship game. Speaking of colleges, check out the California Institute of Technology's **Jet Propulsion Laboratory** *(4800 Oak Grove Ave.; tours by appointment: 818-354-9314).*

The Huntington Library, Art Collections and Botanical Gardens★★★ – *1151 Oxford Rd., San Marino. See Museums* and *Parks and Gardens.*

The Norton Simon Museum★★★ – *411 W. Colorado Blvd. See Museums.*

Gamble House★★ – *4 West Moreland Pl. See Historic Sites.*

An Architectural Feast

More than 600 buildings in Pasadena are on the National Register of Historic Places. For a taste, check out the Civic Center: here you'll find 1920s Spanish Baroque and Renaissance architecture at its finest. The Pasadena Library anchors the north end of the complex. In the center stands **City Hall** *(100 N. Garfield Ave.)*, whose tiled dome is a local landmark. Nearby, the **Pasadena Civic Auditorium** *(300 E. Green St.)*, established in 1931, is the heart of Pasadena's cultural activities and the host of the **People's Choice Awards.** For a complete list of architectural walking tours, check online at: *www.pasadenacal.com.*

The Rose Bowl★

1001 Rose Bowl Dr. 626-577-3100. www.rosebowlstadium.com.

Set on the floor of the Arroyo Seco with spectacular views of the surrounding San Gabriel Mountains, this famed oval stadium (1922, Myron Hunt) can hold 92,542 fans. In addition to hosting the Rose Bowl Game, it's the home stadium for the UCLA football team. *See Musts for Fun.*

Pacific Asia Museum

46 N. Los Robles Ave. 626-449-2742. www.pacificasiamuseum.org. Open Wed–Sun 10am–5pm (Fri until 8pm). $7.

With its upturned roof, flamboyant ornamentation and central courtyard, the two-story 1924 building mimics the Chinese Imperial Palace style. Works in the permanent collection span 5,000 years. Be sure to visit the **Courtyard garden★**, one of only a handful of authentic Chinese gardens in the US.

Pasadena Museum of California Art

490 E. Union St. 626-568-3665. www.pmcaonline.org. Open year-round Wed–Sun 10am–5pm (Fri until 8pm). $6.

Opened in 2002, this three-story museum showcases California art, architecture and design. Its rooftop terrace offers visitors breathtaking **views** of Pasadena City Hall and the San Gabriel Mountains.

Pasadena Museum of History

470 W. Walnut St. at N. Orange Grove Blvd. 626-577-1660. www.pasadenahistory.org. Open year-round Wed–Sun noon–5pm. Tours at 1:30pm & 3pm. $5 admission, $4 tour.

As you wander through the halls of the 18-room Fenyes Estate, former home of the Finnish consul, you'll get a feel for life on "Millionaires' Row" in the early 1900s. On the main floor are original paintings and furnishings; in the basement are photos and historical exhibits. While you're here, stop by the Finnish Folk Art Museum and History Center Galleries, located in what was formerly a sauna.

Pasadena Playhouse – *39 S. El Molino Ave. See Performing Arts.*

San Gabriel Arcángel Mission★

428 S. Mission Dr., San Gabriel. 626-457-3048. www.sangabrielmission.org. Open year-round daily 9am–4:30pm. Closed major holidays. $5. Located about 8mi south of Pasadena, the mission now stands at a bustling suburban intersection. No matter, you can still get a feel for mission life. The **church**, built between 1779 and 1805, is especially noteworthy: reputedly inspired by the Moorish cathedral in Cordoba, Spain, it is composed of 4ft thick adobe walls, supported by capped buttresses.

Downtown★

*Bounded by I-10, I-5, US-101 & Rte. 110. Visitor center at 7th & Figueroa Sts.
www.downtownla.com.*

The massive, multifarious region known as "downtown" encompasses Civic Center, the Business District, and El Pueblo de Los Angeles Historic District. Here you'll find the largest concentration of pre-World War II architecture in the US, in styles ranging from Victorian to Art Deco to post-Modern. If possible, try to peek in the lobbies: you'll find as much variety inside the buildings as you see from the outside. Among downtown's most noteworthy structures are the **Bradbury Building**★★ *(304 S. Broadway)*, the **Eastern Columbia Building**★★ *(849 S. Broadway)* and **Los Angeles City Hall**★★*(200 N. Spring St.). See Landmarks for these and other architectural standouts downtown.*

Getting Around in Downtown LA – Downtown is basically a quadrangle defined by four major highways. Exposition Park and University of Southern California (USC) are in the southwest corner, just south of the Staples Center and the Convention Center. **Little Tokyo** and **Union Station** are in the northeast corner. **Grand Avenue,** the cultural corridor and heart of the business and historic district, runs through Downtown from north to south *(see sidebar below).* The older Beaux-Arts and Art Deco buildings are anchored by Broadway and Spring streets; newer office high rises are clustered between Flower, Hope and Olive streets north of 6th Street. Pico, Olympic and Wilshire Boulevards provide non-freeway access to West LA.

El Pueblo de Los Angeles Historic Monument ★ *– 845 N. Alameda St. See Historic Sites.*

Grand Avenue

Known as LA's "cultural corridor," you'll find tons to see and do on Grand Avenue between West Temple and 6th Streets.

Walt Disney Concert Hall★★★ *– 111 S. Grand Ave. See Landmarks.*

Biltmore Hotel★★ *– 506 S. Grand Ave. See Landmarks.*

California Plaza★ *– 350 S. Grand Ave. See Landmarks.*

Los Angeles Central Library★ *– 630 W. 5th St at Grand Ave. See Landmarks.*

Cathedral of Our Lady of the Angels *– 555 W. Temple St. See Landmarks.*

Music Center of Los Angeles County (includes the Dorothy Chandler Pavilion★, **Ahmanson Theatre and Mark Taper Forum)** *– 135 N. Grand Ave. See Performing Arts.*

Museum of Contemporary Art★★ *– 350 S. Grand Ave. See Museums.*

Little Tokyo

Bounded by 1st & 3rd Sts. and Alameda & Los Angeles Aves. Visitor information: 244 S. San Pedro St.; 213-617-8576; www.jaccc.org.

Los Angeles' Japanese-American community—said to be the largest in the United States—started settling in this seven-block district in 1885. Located southeast of historic City Hall, the area is a bustling business center, shopping district and cultural hub.

The Geffen Contemporary at MOCA★ – *152 N. Central Ave. See Museums.*

James Irvine Garden★ – *244 S. San Pedro St. 213-628-2725. www.jaccc.org. Open year-round daily 9am–5pm. Closed major holidays.* A traditional Japanese land-scape, the 8,500sq ft James Irvine Garden features 30 species of Asian plants. A serene 170ft-long stream symbolizing first-generation Japanese immigrants to America, their children, and their grandchildren (the *issei, nisei* and *sansei*) mean-ders through the park. Overlooking the garden is a large brick plaza, notable for *To the Issei*, a sculpture by Los Angeles native Isamu Noguchi.

Japanese American National Museum★ – *369 E. 1st St. 213-625-0414. www.janm.org. Open year-round Tue–Sun 10am–5pm (Thu until 8pm). Closed major holidays. $6.* This dynamic museum, housed in a former Buddhist temple, presents America's largest inventory of Japanese-American photographs, documents and artifacts.

Japanese Village Plaza – *335 E. 2nd St. 313-620-8861. Great shopping and fine dining.*

Chinatown

Bounded by Alameda, Bernard & Yale Sts. and Sunset Blvd. 213-680-0243. www.chinatownla.com.

Comprising roughly 15 square blocks, LA's Chinatown is relatively small compared to its sprawling San Francisco counterpart. Still, the chinoiserie-bedecked architecture is beautiful, the shopping fun and the restaurants excellent. This is the Chinatown screenwriter Robert Towne had in mind in his film by the same name.

A pagoda-style **gateway** along the 900 block of North Broadway marks the entrance to Gin Ling Way, main street of Central Plaza, Chinatown's original pedestrian precinct.

Chung King Road

The 900 block of Chung King Road is a filled with trendy galleries, which focus on contemporary work by local artists. Here's a sampling:

Mary Goldman – *no. 932; 213-617-8217; www.marygoldman.com.*
China Art Objects – *no. 933; 213-613-0384; www.chinaartobjects.com.*
LMan Gallery – *no. 949; 213-628-3883; www.LMANgallery.com.*
Happy Lion – *no. 963; 213-625-1360; www.thehappylion.com.*
Black Dragon Society – *no. 961; 213-620-0030; www.black-dragon-society.com.*

West Hollywood

Bounded by the Santa Monica Mountains, Hollywood (Melrose Ave.), Los Angeles and Beverly Hills (Doheny Dr). Visitor Information: 800-368-6020 or 310-289-2525; www.visitwesthollywood.com.

The little (1.9sq mi) city of West Hollywood (pop. 36,000) prides itself on being hip, haute, glamorous, fashionable, gay-friendly, design-conscious and beloved by in-the-know celebrities. The city was originally known as Sherman, after Moses Sherman's Los Angeles Pacific Railway Line; it sloughed off that name and took its present one in the early 1920s. By the time it was incorporated in 1984 it was already the cool place it is today.

Sunset Strip ★★

Sunset Blvd., between Doheny Dr. & Crescent Heights Blvd.

This 1.7mi section of Sunset Boulevard was immortalized in the 1960s television series *77 Sunset Strip,* starring Efram Zimbalist, Jr. and Ed Burns. Today the Strip, marked by giant billboards that advertise the latest Hollywood productions, is famed for its bars, restaurants, nightclubs and shopping *(see Must Shop, Must Eat,* and *Nightlife).*

In January 2004 the **Architecture and Design (A+D) Museum**, formerly located in downtown LA, opened in the former Playboy Building at the new Sunset Millennium Project *(8560 Sunset Blvd.; 310-659-2445; www.aplusd.org; open year-round Mon–Fri 9am–6pm).* It presents rotating exhibits.

Long a hideaway for the glitterati, the stately **Chateau Marmont** *(8221 Sunset Blvd.; 323-656-1010; www.chateaumarmont.com),* a seven-story amalgam of Norman and Moorish influences, rises above the Strip's easternmost end.

Museum of Contemporary Art ★★ – *8687 Melrose Ave. See Museums.*

Melrose Avenue ★ – *See Must Shop.*

Avenues of Art & Design – *310-289-2534. www.avenuesartdesign.com.*
This collection of upscale design shops and more than 30 art galleries flanks Melrose Avenue, Beverly and Robertson boulevards.

Argyle Hotel ★

8358 Sunset Blvd. 323-654-7100 or 800-225-2637. www.argylehotel.com.

Originally known as the Sunset Towers Apartments, this National Historic Landmark was completed in 1929 and was home to such stars as Errol Flynn, Clark Gable, Jean Harlow, Bob Hope and John Wayne. In 1985, the Argyle was restored to its original grandeur and decorated with reproductions from the Beaux-Arts Museum in Paris and the Metropolitan Museum of Art in New York City. **Fenix** at the Argyle serves European and New American cuisine.

Los Angeles has 70 miles of sandy beaches, attracting a continuous parade of walkers, runners, joggers, cyclists, Roller-bladers, surfers and sunbathers. Work your way down the shore or zoom in on the following highlights.

Long Beach★

30mi south of LA via I-405 & I-710. Tourist information: 562-436-3645 or www.visitlongbeach.com.

Long Beach, linked to downtown LA by the Metro blue line, enjoys a close connection to the sea. Backbone of the local economy, its port is one of the largest and busiest in the world, and its waterfront just got a $300 million sprucing-up.

Queen Mary★★★

1126 Queens Hwy. 562-435-3511. www.queenmary.com. Open daily 10am–6pm. $23 self-guided. $28 guided tour (recommended) and admission to adjacent submarine.

A visit to this storied ocean liner, a floating museum bigger than the ill-fated Titanic, will make you think twice next time you get on a plane. Convenience?

Economy? Bah . . . Built in England, the *Queen Mary* was a wonder of grace and efficiency. She set off on her maiden voyage in May 1936. No dawdler, she was the fastest ship of her time, with a cruising speed of up to 40mph. For three years she catered to the crème de la crème: All 800 first-class passengers could eat at once, in the largest room ever built on a ship. The wine cellar stocked 15,000 bottles. Guest rooms and lounges were paneled in exotic tropical hardwoods in the latest Art Deco designs, and decks were made of polished teak.

With the onset of World War II, the Queen Mary was conscripted into military duty. Between 1939 and 1946, she carried 750,000 troops a distance of over 550,000 miles, earning the nickname "the Gray Ghost" for her uncanny ability to slip past destroyers and subs. In 1947 she was returned to civilian use, completing a total of 1,001 transatlantic voyages before coming to rest here in 1967.

Scorpion Submarine★ – Moored next to the ship, the 3,000-ton Soviet vessel (1972) offers a considerably more cramped version of ocean going. Tour the torpedo rooms, officers' and seamen's quarters, sonar room, control room, galley and engine compartments.

Stay a little longer . . .

. . . and enjoy more of what the Queen Mary has to offer:

Queen Mary Hotel – Rooms from the porthole-less to the luxurious from $109.

Observation Bar – Nightly cocktails, live music, and dancing in the original first-class bar, an Art Deco masterpiece.

Sunday Champagne Brunch – An international buffet in the Grand Salon. *Reservations: 562-499-1506.*

Long Beach Aquarium of the Pacific★★

100 Aquarium Way, off Shoreline Dr. 562-590-3100. www.aquariumofpacific.org. Open year-round daily 9am–6pm. Closed Apr 1, during the weekend of the Toyota Grand Prix of Long Beach in mid-Apr, & Dec 25. $18.95 ($34 including Queen Mary admission).

The flowing, wavelike structure (the baffle is unique in the world) holds one of the most comprehensive marine-themed exhibitions in California. Its canvas is the Pacific Ocean, represented by more than 12,500 creatures.

Northern Pacific – See the ever-frisky sea otters; puffins and other diving birds; and giant spider crabs, octopi and starfish.

Shark Lagoon – The aquarium's newest exhibit features 150 sharks, some of which you can touch.

Southern California and Baja – Critters include seals and sea lions, leopard sharks and barracuda, and ancient sea turtles.

Tropical Pacific – Ogle the dazzling living coral lagoon and the barrier reef.

Rainbow Harbor

On Shoreline Dr. www.rainbowharbor.com.

This new $300-million waterfront district stretches from the aquarium on its west end to **Shoreline Village**★, a carnival-like complex of shops, on its east end. At the heart of the project is the **harbor**★ itself, home to pleasure craft, fishing boats, cruise boats, tall ships, and even a Mississippi steamboat. The 350,000sq ft **Pike at Rainbow Harbor**, completed in 2004, has stadium-style movie theaters, a bowling alley, an arcade and lots of shops and restaurants.

San Pedro

Just across the stately **Vincent Thomas Bridge** from Long Beach, the town of San Pedro was Southern California's main harbor community throughout the 1800s. Annexed to LA in 1909, it's now home to the massive **Worldport LA** freight and passenger terminal and to beautiful **Cabrillo Beach,** and **Ports O'Call,** a New England–style village with shops, restaurants and other diversions *(see Musts for Fun).*

Cabrillo Marine Aquarium – *3720 Stephen White Dr. off Pacific Ave. Open year-round Tue–Fri noon–5pm; weekends 10am–5pm. 310-548-7562. www.cabrilloaq.org.* Award-winning architect Frank Gehry designed the building for this small aquarium, which opened in 1981. Thirty-eight saltwater aquariums display Southern California sea creatures, including sharks, eels, octopi and crabs in natural environments.

Malibu★

Exclusive Malibu stretches along some 27mi of coastline where the Santa Monica Mountains abruptly meet the Pacific. It's known for its beautiful beaches, many sheltered by dramatic cliffs; spectacular sunsets; and celebrity residents. Mudslides and forest fires occasionally denude its slopes and destroy a few mansions, but few who can afford it are dissuaded from rebuilding.

In 1928 developer Art Jones established **Malibu Colony,** a residential enclave for the Hollywood elite: Clara Bow, Gary Cooper and Gloria Swanson all ponied up $1 per square foot per month (expensive even by today's prices) to live in the beachside abodes. Today it's a gated community with a similarly well-heeled, star-studded clientele.

Arrayed along the Pacific Coast Highway—"PCH" to locals—Malibu's restaurants, cafes and shops attract a mix of beachgoers, locals, tourists and glitterati.

J. Paul Getty Villa

17985 Pacific Coast Hwy. Closed for renovation until fall 2005. Check Web site for updates: www.getty.edu.

One of this century's wealthiest businessmen, Getty had impeccable taste for art and he knew how to show it to best advantage. This spectacular site is a lushly landscaped 65-acre canyon overlooking the Pacific; the villa replicates a pre-Christian Roman abode buried in the lava of Mt. Vesuvius. In 1997 the villa closed and the art was moved to the celebrated **Getty Center★★★** in LA *(see Museums).* When it reopens, it will house the Getty's vast collection of Greek and Roman antiquities.

Malibu Beaches★

Malibu has plenty of beaches to choose from, from serious surfer hangouts to secluded romantic coves. *Beaches are listed from south to north as you're headed up the Pacific Coast Hwy. Go to www.malibu.org for a list of amenities at each site.*

Surfrider County Beach★ – This is a favorite spot for volleyball, sunbathing, fishing and, of course, surfing.

Zuma Beach – *Lifeguard station: 310-457-2525.* Zuma is Malibu's biggest and most popular beach.

La Piedra, El Matador, and El Pescador Beaches – These secluded coves or cliff-foot strands are known locally as "pocket beaches."

Leo Carrillo State Beach – This big, sandy beach is thronged with windsurfers, kite surfers, and just regular surfers.

Santa Monica★

Tourist information: 310-393-7593 or www.santamonica.com.

Sunny Santa Monica borders the Pacific Ocean 13mi west of downtown Los Angeles. Dubbed the "Zenith City of the Sunset Seas" in the 1870s, it's a thriving, upscale place with lots of healthy-looking tanned people and plenty of palm trees.

In the late 19C, Santa Monica was briefly considered as a site for LA's port, but locals fought the measure (the port went to San Pedro) and developed their town as a summer retreat. The Santa Monica Pier—the oldest pleasure pier on the West Coast—opened in 1909. The city remained relatively low-key until 1966, when the completion of the Santa Monica Freeway (I-10) brought a tidal wave of new development. Today this year-round urban beach town boasts high-caliber art galleries, chic shops, a wide sandy beach and smart oceanfront hotels.

> **Did You Know?**
>
> Legend has it that the city's name was coined in the 18C by Spanish missionaries, who likened the trickling water of its natural springs to the 40 tears of St. Monica as she mourned her heretical son, Augustine.

Santa Monica Pier★★

Western end of Colorado Ave.

Jutting some 1,000ft over the ocean, the pier has an old-time carnival feel, with an antique **carousel**★, curio shops and other amusements. There are actually two structures here, the Municipal Pier (1909) and the Pleasure Pier (1916); the latter was designed by Coney Island creator Charles I.D. Looff. *See Musts for Kids.*

Palisades Park

The park stretches along a sandstone bluff on the beach side of Ocean Avenue from Colorado Avenue to the Malibu border at Adelaide Drive. Extraordinary sunset **views**★★ are enhanced at *Palisades Gestation III*, the large abstract seed pod positioned so that the winter solstice sunset is perfectly framed within the sculpture's opening.

Third Street Promenade★, Bergamot Station Arts Center★, and Santa Monica Farmers' Market – *See Must Shop*.

Venice★

www.venicebeach.com.

When tobacco magnate Abbot Kinney first developed his "Venice of America," in 1904–1905, it wasn't quite so diverse as it is today. In those days, Mary Pickford rowed her personal gondola in Kinney's Venetian-styled canals (now mostly filled in), Charlie Chaplin clowned in Kinney's auto races, and William Randolph Hearst and Marion Davies strolled the Venice boardwalk, still the town's most popular attraction.

Venice Beach★★ – One of California's most popular beaches is renowned not only for its sand and surf but for its colorful street life, particularly along **Ocean Front Walk,** a beachside walkway lined with outdoor cafes and trinket shops. On sunny days it's packed with vacationers and vagrants, chic Angelenos and trendy teens, entrepreneurial palm readers and psychics, and roller-skating rap artists. Recently restored pagodas offer both shade and seating.

Abbot Kinney Boulevard – *See Must Shop.*

Marina del Rey

Tourist information: 310-306-9900 or www.visitthemarina.com.

The "Marina," as its name implies, is a community built for and around boats. Home to 9,000 vessels, it has the largest man-made small-boat harbor in the world and, nearby, the highest density of restaurant seating per one-square-mile of any place outside Manhattan—presumably to feed hungry seafarers. Here are some ideas for getting out on the water:

Marina Boat Rentals – *13719 Fiji Way. 310 574-2822. www.boats-4rent.com.* For a short jaunt, try renting a boat. For staying close to shore, try a one-person kayak *($12/hr)* or a Jet Ski *($90/hr)*; 17ft Flare runabouts for the harbor go for $50/hr. For an ocean-going vessel, expect to spend between $70 and $90 an hour.

Hornblower Cruises and Events – *Fisherman's Village. 310-306-9474. www.hornblower.com.* Harbor cruises include a glass of champagne, a three-course sit-down meal, plus music and dancing *(Fri 7:30pm–10:30pm, $59.95/person; Sat 7pm–10pm, $65.95/person).*

Paradise-Bound Yacht Charters – *Ritz-Carlton hotel, 4375 Admiralty Way. 800-655-0850. www.the-calculating-lady.com/captalex.* Take a sunset, coastal or Catalina Island cruise on any of a range of vessels, from a two-person submarine to a 42ft sailboat or motor yacht. Gourmet catering is available.

South Bay Beaches

All three of these "back in the day" beach towns—Manhattan Beach, Hermosa Beach and Redondo Beach—have a small-town feel, typifying the Southland's love of casual living. Twenty miles southwest of downtown, they took on their present character in the 1950s, when defense dollars flooded California. Today their streets are lined with ranch- and Spanish Colonial-style houses—many within walking distance of the beach.

Manhattan Beach – The most upscale of the South Bay communities, Manhattan Beach lies 19mi south of LA. It claims a landmark 928ft-long pier, lots of tiny bungalows, charming Victorian homes, 2mi of beach frontage, 48 acres of parkland, and an abundance of eateries, mostly along Manhattan Beach Boulevard and Manhattan and Highland avenues.

Hermosa Beach – *www.hermosabch.org.* This pier-front city is popular with surfers, swimmers, jazz and comedy aficionados. *Los Angeles Magazine* named it an "outstanding coastal town" for its lodgings, shops and restaurants.

Redondo Beach – Monstad Pier is the biggest boardwalk between Santa Monica and San Pedro.

Zazou

1810 S. Catalina Ave., Manhattan Beach. 310-540-4884. www.ezazou.com. Open for lunch and dinner Tue–Sat. Just a block away from the beach, this little gem serves up creative fare at easy-on-the-pocketbook prices. Blending American, French and Middle Eastern influences, Zazou's ever-changing menu features such creative dishes as salmon with artichoke a la Grecque, and ricotta-pumpkin gnocchi with rock shrimp and fava beans. Chef/owner Guy Gabriele calls it "cuisine of the sun." Diners call it delicious.

The stars, the stunts, the shoots, the special effects. It all happens in LA's film studios. To get the inside scoop, take a tour—who knows which stars you'll see? On one recent NBC tour, Ellen Degeneres was the oh-so-silly page; at Universal, Jim Carrey chased trams in full Grinch makeup.

Studio tours are a mix of movie history, behind-the-scenes' secrets and sheer entertainment. Though "Hollywood" production takes place throughout the city, most studios are located in the San Fernando Valley. In fact, the area has been home to so many television shows and motion pictures that there are plaques along Ventura Boulevard to celebrate each one.

Universal Studios Hollywood★★★

100 Universal City Plaza, Universal City. 818-508-9600. www.universalstudioshollywood. com. Open Mon–Fri 9am–6pm, weekends & summer 9am–10pm. $49 general admission. $39 for children under 48 inches; free for children under age 3. $8 parking.

What started in 1964 as a train ride to boost lunch-time revenues at the Universal Studios' commissary has mushroomed into a sprawling enter-tainment complex where visitors can "ride the movies." Universal Studios Hollywood covers 420 acres across a hillside overlooking the San Fernando Valley, 3mi northwest of Hollywood Boulevard. The world's largest movie studio and theme park, Universal hosts more than 5 million visitors each year.

> **Tips for Visiting**
>
> Adventure seekers should head straight for the park's most popular thrill rides: **Shrek: 4-D**; **Terminator 2: 3D**; **Jurassic Park—The Ride;** and **Backdraft**. A new indoor roller coaster, **Revenge of the Mummy—The Ride**, debuts in summer 2004.

Studio Center – Lights, camera, action! Situated in and around Universal's actual sound stages and back lots, the lower section of the park features fantasy villages, theme restaurants and a bevy of shops. Where else can you visit the Old West, Cape Cod, Baker Street, a row of New York City brown-stones, and a Parisian courtyard—all in one day?

Must Ride

Shrek: 4-D – Join everybody's favorite ogre and his princess bride on their rollicking 3-D honeymoon.

Terminator 2: 3D – Arnold's back with a vengeance in the gripping film that marries stunt work, special effects and in-your-face 3-D technology.

Jurassic Park—The Ride – A pleasant river cruise turns into a harrowing ride as T-Rex rears his ugly head.

Van Helsing: Fortress Dracula – Immerse yourself in the dark world of Dracula, Frankenstein and the Wolf Man—if you dare. This attraction debuted in May 2004 along with the Stephen Sommer thriller.

Revenge of the Mummy—The Ride – Opening in summer 2004, this indoor roller coaster will take you on a thrilling journey through the gruesome Egyptian underworld.

Universal Studios Hollywood Studio Tour ★★

What really goes on behind the scenes on a movie set? Hop aboard a tram at the Universal Entertainment Center, and find out. As the tram meanders through the back lots, you'll get a brief history of Universal's film and television productions, beginning with how silent-film producer Carl Laemmle converted a 230-acre chicken ranch into the Universal Film Manufacturing Company in 1915. The tour passes 35 soundstages, where you'll see movie sets, props, lights, cameras—and maybe even action—not to mention all the behind-the-scenes contributions to filmmaking. All is not as calm as it seems, however. En route, you'll encounter **King Kong** and survive an **Earthquake**.

Universal CityWalk® ★

818-622-4455. www.citywalkhollywood.com

From shopping to dining to club-hopping, you'll find fun for the whole family at this popular entertainment complex, where you can experience Hollywood at its trendiest. While the kids are wearing themselves out at **Nickelodeon Blast Zone**, parents can prepare for a night out by purchasing a **Nighttime Party Pass** *($16)*, which offers all-club access within CityWalk.

CityWalk Shopping

CityWalk stores cater to Gen-Xers with Red Balls (alternative clothing), Billabong (togs for board sports), and Abercrombie & Fitch. Universal Studios Store and The Raider Image are good places to buy souvenirs for the folks back home. When you need a breather, stop in at Zen Zone's oxygen bar—and be sure you *do* inhale.

Warner Bros. Studios★

4000 Warner Blvd., Burbank. 818-846-1403. www.studio-tour.com. VIP Tour Mon–Fri 9am–3pm (until 4pm in summer). $32. Deluxe Tour ($95) includes lunch in the studio dining room.

You'll feel like a VIP on this small-group (limited to 15 people) tour once restricted to the most celebrated personalities. The journey begins with a short film highlighting the studio's accomplishments over the years. Then, you'll proceed to the **Warner Bros. Museum**, which houses a large collection of movie memorabilia, including four best-picture Oscars, costumes, props and complete movie scripts. From here, you'll be guided through the back lot sets, soundstages and craft shops.

- **New York Street** should seem familiar, as *Batman, Lois & Clark* and the TV series *ER* were all filmed there.

- If you're a *Gilmore Girls* fan, be sure to note **Midwest Street,** the show's studio location.

- The **Western back lot** has been home over the years to *Bonanza, Little House on the Prairie* and *Maverick.*

Depending on what's going on while you're visiting, you may also get to visit **The Mill,** which has served as Warner Bros.' craft shop for nearly 75 years, or learn the secrets of sound-editing on a Foley stage.

NBC Studios

3000 W. Alameda Ave., Burbank. 818-840-3537 or 818-840-4444. www.studioaudiences.com. Tours Mon–Fri 9am–3pm. Phone for current schedule and extended summer hours. $7.50.

To get a behind-the-scenes perspective on TV productions for a modest price, visit NBC studios. Currently the only commercial TV network offering studio tours, NBC takes you on a 70-minute, indoor walking tour that offers a no-frills glimpse of a working television studio.

As you amble along the tour path, you'll pass the sets of *Days of our Lives* and *Salem Place*. You'll discover the secrets behind special effects when one of your group is chosen to "fly" like Superman; and you'll learn about sound effects as participants in the tour's *Trivia Time* game show.

Along the way, you'll also see the vast warehouse areas where props are stored, and watch craftsmen hard at work building realistic sets. You'll walk past the commissary, get a peek at the NBC wardrobe department and even visit the set of *The Tonight Show with Jay Leno*.

See A Live TV Show

Have you always wanted to be part of a live TV audience? Well, here's your chance. You can watch the stars without paying for an expensive tour by joining the studio audience for a live or taped TV show. Here are some good places to get tickets:

Audience Associates, Inc. – *323-653-4105. www.tvtix.com*. This group offers free tickets to a number of game shows, sitcoms and talk shows for all major networks.

Audiences Unlimited, Inc. – *818-753-3470. www.tvtickets.com*. Located near Universal Studio Walk, Audiences Unlimited represents over 35 network comedies filmed in LA and offers free tickets to anyone wanting to be part of the studio audience.

NBC – *818-840-3438. www.nbc.com*. Tickets for the *Tonight Show with Jay Leno* can be obtained in advance. For tickets to other NBC shows, go to the NBC Ticket Box Office *(3000 W. Alameda Ave., Burbank; office opens at 8am)* on the day of the show, or contact one of the general ticket providers.

Paramount – *323-956-1777. www.paramount.com*. You can get tickets to several shows, including *Becker,* by calling the information line. Paramount also provides tickets for *Dr. Phil*, which can be reserved online or by phone *(323-461-7445)*.

Paramount Pictures Studio

5555 Melrose Ave., Hollywood. 323-956-5000. www.paramount.com. Recognizable by the wrought-iron **studio gates** at the corner of Bronson Avenue and Marathon Street, Paramount Pictures, which moved to its current location in 1926, is the oldest continually running studio in Hollywood. The enormous complex, whose landmark water tower still looms above the back lots, once claimed its own fire department and hospital. More than 3,000 movies have been produced at Paramount, including *Forrest Gump* (1994), *White Christmas* (1954) and *The Godfather* (1972). Although the studio ceased its tours following the terrorist attacks on September 11, 2001, it still offers tickets to television shows *(see above)*.

Television Ticket Co. – *818-688-3974. www.freetvshows.com*. This company has free tickets to a number of hit shows, including *The Wayne Brady Show* and FoxSports' *Best Damn Sports Show Period.*

Universal Studios Hollywood – *818-508-9600. www.universalstudioshollywood.com*. At Universal, you can reserve seats for television shows, and sign up for parts in crowd scenes, commercials, movies, and television shows.

Museums

Pop culture may get most of the media attention, but you'll find more museums per capita in Los Angeles than in any city in the world. Three hundred venues in LA focus on themes as ethereal as art, as relevant as science, and as important as history and social justice. Here are a few of our favorites.

Getty Center★★★

1200 Getty Center Dr., just off I-405. 310-440-7300. www.getty.edu. Open year-round Sun & Tue–Thu 10am–6pm, Fri–Sat 10am–9pm. Closed Mon & major holidays. Parking reservations required Mon–Fri (see Tips for Visiting, below). $5/parking.

Perched on a north-south ridge high above the San Diego Freeway, a gleaming cluster of low-lying buildings holds one of the nation's most extensive facilities for the study, conservation and presentation of visual art.

The only child of oil magnate George F. Getty, **Jean Paul Getty** (1892–1976) worked for a living—which is to say, by the age of 23 he had become fabulously wealthy in his own right, by investing his millions in Oklahoma oil fields. He began collecting paintings in 1931, and after World War II he spent most of his

time in Europe both on business (running the oil company) and for pleasure (collecting antiquities and other art). Originally his holdings were displayed in Malibu. But under the direction of the vast J. Paul Getty Trust—reputedly the largest museum endowment in the world—they soon needed a bigger space for proper display.

American architect Richard Meier won the commission to design the new facility, with spectacular results: the travertine-clad, 24-acre complex melds six buildings with courtyards, walkways, fountains and gardens and affords stunning views.

Tips for Visiting

Because the museum is balanced on a high ridge, you can't get to it by car—at least not directly. Cleverly, they have you park at the base of the hill and ascend to the museum in a cool electric tram. Up top, the glass-walled Entrance Hall is the functional heart of the museum for visitors. The information desk, to the left, has floor plans as well as schedules of lectures, docent tours and other activities. To the right, you can rent tape-recorded gallery tours for $3. Take 10 minutes to watch the orientation film, shown on a continuous loop throughout the day.

North Pavilion – *Art before 1600; plaza level.* Exhibitions cover 16C European bronzes; 15C–16C European ceramics (Spanish floor tiles, lusterware and sculpture); and German and Italian glassware. The highlight of the floor is the outstanding collection of **illuminated manuscripts★★**. Upstairs are Italian Renaissance paintings by Fra Bartolommeo, Pontormo, Titian and Veronese.

East Pavilion – *Art from 1600 to 1800.* On the plaza level are European sculpture and drawings from the Renaissance through the Rococo periods, most produced in Italian, Flemish or German workshops. Paintings on the upper level include works by Jan Brueghel the Elder, Valentin de Boulogne and Rembrandt van Rijn *(Old Man in Military Costume,* c.1630, and *St. Bartholomew,* 1661).

South Pavilion – *Art from 1600 to 1800.* On the plaza level you'll find monumental French tapestries from the period of Louis XIV and an entire gallery of tables, clocks, chests and other decorative items attributed to marquetry master André-Charles Boulle. Four paneled rooms show the evolving tastes of interior decor between 1670 and 1795. Upstairs are works by Thomas Gainsborough, Jean-Baptiste Simeon Chardin and other famous European artists.

West Pavilion – *Art after 1800.* Changing displays of European sculpture, along with rotating exhibits of photography, adorn the lower level, while above you'll find some of the best-known works by Impressionist painters. Van Gogh's *Irises,* dating from 1889, is perhaps the museum's most famous work.

Gardens – Robert Irwin's 110-acre Central Garden crosses a ravine between the main museum and the Research Institute and incorporates a tree-lined walkway, 500 plant species and a waterfall. On the south promontory, the Cactus Garden offers a marvelous **view★** across Greater Los Angeles.

J. Paul Getty Villa – *17985 Pacific Coast Hwy., Malibu. Closed for renovation until fall 2005. See Beach Communities.*

Portrait of Alfonso d'Avalos, Marchese del Vasto

In November 2003 the Getty illustrated its growing power in the art world by acquiring an influential Titian portrait. Completed in the first few months of 1533, the painting is a stunningly rendered, half-length depiction of Alfonso d'Avalos, a Neapolitan nobleman, intellectual and art collector. Getty curators were drawn to its composition ("figures emerge from a cocoon of indeterminate yet tangible space as if sculpted in three dimensions") and character ("D'Avalos' features and introspective expression are insightfully and sensitively described"). The $70-million price tag makes it the second-most expensive Old Master purchase in history.

Huntington Library, Art Collections and Botanical Gardens★★★

1151 Oxford Rd., San Marino. 626-405-2141. www.huntington.org. Open year-round May–Sept Tue–Sun 10:30am–4:30pm. Rest of the year Tue–Fri noon–4:30pm, weekends 10:30am–4:30pm. Closed Mon & holidays. $12.50.

When you tour the palatial home and gardens of railroad magnate **Henry Huntington** (1850–1927) and his second wife Arabella, you feel as if you are in another, French-inspired world. Huntington built his Beaux-Arts mansion in 1910 on land that was originally a 500-acre winery. At the age of 60, he decided to devote his life to acquiring art and books and to creating a premier botanical garden. Three years later he married Arabella, his uncle's widow, a francophile and an avid art collector. Her influence extended to the art, the period furnishings and the sculptures in the gardens.

Through the years, Huntington, who invested in real estate (Huntington Beach), sold off parcels to purchase great art; today there are 150 acres of gardens on a 207-acre, immaculately appointed estate. The mausoleum, which was used as the prototype for the Jefferson Memorial in Washington, DC (and has been seen in films to represent it), is among the most significant architectural buildings at this remarkable cultural attraction. Each year, more than 2,000 scholars do research at the Huntington and more than 500,000 people visit—including about 25,000 school children in docent-led groups.

Botanical Gardens★★– *See Parks and Gardens.*

Library★★ – Tagged as "the Bastille of Books," the library at the Huntington is one of the most complete research libraries in the United States. Built in 1920 to house an outstanding collection, it contains more than 5 million items in its areas of specialization that are available to researchers. Among its treasures, there's a copy of the 15C Gutenberg Bible on vellum, an unsurpassed collection of the early editions of Shakespeare's works, the Ellesmere manuscript of Chaucer's *Canterbury Tales* and the double-elephant folio edition of *Audubon's Birds of America*. Among the manuscripts there are original letters by Geroge Washington, Thomas Jefferson, Benjamin Franklin and Abraham Lincoln. The Library Exhibition Hall is open to the public.

Huntington Art Gallery★★

Located within the original Huntington residence, this impressive Beaux-Arts structure contains an extraordinary trove of 18C and 19C British and French art.

British Collection★★★ – Located in the main gallery, this collection is considered among the finest outside of London, particularly for its grouping of 20 life-size, full-length 18C portraits by Sir Joshua Reynolds *(Sarah Siddons as the Tragic Muse)*, Thomas Gainsborough *(Jonathan Buttall: "The Blue Boy")* and Sir Thomas Lawrence *(Sarah Barrett Moulton: "Pinkie")*. The adjoining passage displays a collection of English miniature portraits (late 16C to early 19C), along with early-16C silver. Elsewhere in the two-story building you'll find paintings, drawings and sculpture in rooms richly appointed with 18C English and French furnishings.

Arabella Huntington Memorial Collection – Nestled in the west wing of the library are Renaissance paintings, 18C French sculpture, a rare collection of pristine Beauvais tapestries, porcelain and furniture. Rogier van der Weyden's 15C masterpiece *Madonna and Child* is considered to be the most important painting in the collection.

George and MaryLou Boone Gallery – The 1911 carriage house presents changing exhibits of American and English art, rare books and manuscripts.

Virginia Steele Scott Gallery – This gallery opened in 1984 and is devoted to American art. It includes works by Mary Cassatt, John Singleton Copley and John Singer Sargent. Appropriate to Pasadena, there's an exhibit of decorative Arts and Crafts pieces and room settings by Pasadena-based architects Charles and Henry Greene. This is part of the Greene & Greene Center for the Study of the Arts and Crafts

Movement in America, a project jointly sponsored by The Huntington and the **Gamble House**★★ *(see Historic Sites)*.

A Night at the Huntington

626-405-2128, www.huntington.org. Occasional Saturdays 6:30–9:30pm. Call for schedule. Kids of all ages delight in watching nature come alive after dark in the Huntington's celebrated botanical gardens. Docents will lead you through the greenery, where you can spot night-blooming plants and see nocturnal animals from Wildlife on Wheels. Then you can turn your eyes skyward as LA Astronomy Society members let you gaze at the heavens through telescopes.

Los Angeles County Museum of Art ★★★

5905 Wilshire Blvd. 323-857-6000. www.lacma.org. Open year-round Mon–Tue & Thu noon–8pm; Fri noon–9pm; weekends 11am–8pm. Closed Wed, Thanksgiving Day & Dec 25. $9.

LA's all-purpose art museum is the largest in the country west of Chicago, with 150,000 works dating from ancient Egypt right up to the present. It's also one of the youngest.

LACMA, as locals like to call it, was originally part of the Museum of History, Science, and Art, which opened in 1913 in Exposition Park. The art department peeled off on its own in 1961 and opened three years later in the sprawling six-building complex at the heart of "Miracle Mile," as this stretch of Wilshire is called. The first three imposing structures were built by Pereira & Assocs.; the fourth, by Hardy Holzman Pfeiffer, was completed in 1986; its monumental façade of limestone, glass blocks and green-glazed terra-cotta echoes the Art Deco aesthetic of the neighborhood. The 1988 opening of the curvilinear Pavilion for Japanese Art, by Bruce Goff and Bart Prince, underscored the city's ties to the East.

Ahmanson Building

This four-level structure houses the largest share of LACMA's permanent collection, displayed in galleries off the central atrium.

Plaza Level – Here you'll find African art, mostly from the 20C, and pre-Columbian works from Mexico and Central America. In the American Decorative Arts Collection, note works by Gustav Stickley, Tiffany and the Herter Bros. American Painting and Sculpture from the 18C to the early 20C includes works by O'Keeffe, Homer, Cassatt, Sargent, and members of the Ashcan and Hudson River schools.

Second Level – Take in the sweeping survey of ancient Egyptian, Iranian, Greek and Roman art. The Renaissance and Mannerist collections highlight works by Titian, Tintoretto, Vasari, Veronese and El Greco. Rembrandt, Frans Hals and Rubens are among the 17C Dutch and Flemish artists represented.

A passageway leads to the **Hammer Building** and its wonderful samples of Impressionist and post-Impressionist works by Cézanne, Degas, Gauguin, Monet, Pissarro, Renoir and Toulouse-Lautrec.

Third Level – Composed of approximately 35,000 paintings, sculptures, ceramics, textiles and works of silver, jade and crystal, the collection of Islamic, Southeast Asian, Indian, Tibetan and Nepalese art is considered one of three finest in the world.

Robert O. Anderson Building

This is where you'll find some supreme samples of 20C masters such as Pablo Picasso, Frank Stella, René Magritte and Isamu Noguchi. Worth noting on the second level, which features post-1960 art, is the lushly impressionistic rendering of the Hollywood Hills in *Mulholland Drive: The Road to the Studio* (1980), by the English-born, Los Angeles-based artist David Hockney.

Sculpture Gardens

Two outdoor sculpture gardens flank the Anderson Building on Wilshire Boulevard and showcase large works by major sculptors. The garden on the west side displays bronzes by Rodin and can be accessed via the Central Court. Nine works—including ones by Alexander Calder and Henry Moore—are immediately to the right of the Wilshire Boulevard entrance.

Pavilion for Japanese Art

The structure reminds some of the Guggenheim Museum in New York because of its appealing spiraling space. Natural light filters through Lucite walls made to approximate rice-paper *shoji* screens, and waterfalls create soothing white noise. The design is a particularly effective way to show off the Shin-enkan collection donated to LACMA by Joe D. Price and his Japanese-born wife, Etsuko, in 1982: the more than 300 scroll paintings and screens created during Japan's Edo period represent the finest collection of its kind in the Western world.

LACMA West

6067 Wilshire Blvd. at Fairfax Ave.

The former May Co. Department Store, a dramatic 1939 Streamline Moderne edifice, became LACMA West in 1998. Its 4,000sq ft of gallery space houses an impressive collection of Latin American Art, along with special exhibitions and the Boone Children's Gallery.

And . . . Roll 'Em!

Attend a screening at LACMA's Bing Theater while you're in town. The ticket price *($8 evenings; $2 matinees)* includes gallery admission as well. Films vary from Hollywood new releases to Cannes Film Festival winners to award-winning British television commercials. Every Tuesday at 1pm, LACMA plucks a classic film from the Warner Bros./ Turner Entertainment Company library. Tickets may be purchased at the entrance to the Bing Theater 30 minutes before showtime. *For schedules, go to the Central Court information booth, call 323-857-6010, or check online at www.lacma.org.*

Norton Simon Museum★★★

411 W. Colorado Blvd., Pasadena. 626-449-6840. www.nortonsimon.org. Open year-round Wed–Mon noon–6pm, Fri noon–9pm. $6.

You may recognize this low-rise, curvilinear modern building as the backdrop for the start of the Tournament of Roses Parade without knowing that inside is one of the most remarkable collections of art ever assembled. The museum, founded in 1924 as the Pasadena Art Institute, opened as the Pasadena Art Museum in 1969 and was reorganized in 1974 under the direction of industrialist Norton Simon.

With deep pockets and an incredible eye for art, Simon was one of America's greatest 20C art collectors. He started amassing his collection in the 1950s. Within two decades he owned a range of the best European art: works by Old Masters, such as Rembrandt and Goya (Goya's *Disasters of War* is one of only twelve printed during his lifetime); Impressionists and post-Impressionists, such as Manet, Degas, and Cézanne; and 20C geniuses like Matisse, Picasso and Klimt. When Simon's wife, Jennifer Jones, introduced him to the beauty of India, he amassed an array of Asian art that spans 2,000 years.

First Floor – After Architect Frank Gehry completed a redesign, renovation and expansion of the museum's 51,000sq ft of gallery space, the *New York Times* reported that "the Simon collection has never looked better." Inside the entry, Gehry puts you within viewing range of Van Gogh paintings and some of the clay models Degas used for his dance and horse bronzes

(they number more than 70). The design then draws you through a courtyard of Rodin sculptures into a foyer where you can see the transformed sculpture garden and some of the best artworks in the museum.

Lower Level – You come to the Asian art and artifacts via a curving stairwell that opens onto what feels like an ancient temple. One Buddha is positioned at the end of a corridor in front of a glass-fronted outdoor garden. It's a setting that's as verdant as a South Seas painting by Henri Rousseau.

Sculpture garden

Designed by noted landscape designer Nancy Goslee Power, the garden features California plantings and pays homage to Monet's Giverny with a water-lily-studded pond, and to Van Gogh with a flowerbed of irises.

Museum of Contemporary Art★★

250 S. Grand Ave. 213-626-6222. www.moca.org. Open year-round Mon & Fri 11am–5pm, Thu 11am–8pm (free); weekends 11am–6pm. Closed Tue, Wed & major holidays. $8 (valid for all MOCA locations).

As you walk here from the Music Center or the adjacent California Plaza, you'll see MOCA's distinctive pyramids, cubes, and cylinders. Japanese architect Arata Isozaki designed the red sandstone building, which opened in December 1986. From the ticket booth, a boxy construction paneled in green aluminum and outlined in a bright pink diamond pattern, look up to the copper-sheathed barrel-vaulted roofline that covers the library and at the delicately veined onyx in the arched window. The multilevel outdoor space has a waterfall and an outdoor cafe. A sweeping staircase leads from street level to the sunken entry court, where you'll find 24,500sq ft of gallery space lit by pyramidal skylights.

Visit – The permanent collection of more than 5,000 artworks are rendered in all imaginable media. Big names such as Diane Arbus, Andy Warhol, Mark Rothko, Jackson Pollock, Franz Kline, Alberto Giacometti share the bill with mid-career artists and up-and-comers. More than 20 traveling exhibits are also shown here each year.

Geffen Contemporary at MOCA★

152 N. Central Ave. 213-626-6222. www.moca-la.org. Open year-round Tue–Sun 11am–5pm (Thu 8pm). Closed Jan 1, July 4, Thanksgiving Day & Dec 25.

The ubiquitous Frank Gehry transformed this 45,000sq ft former warehouse complex into an exhibition space before MOCA's "new" home was completed in 1986, earning it the sobriquet "the Temporary Contemporary." Now it's permanent. Look for artists such as Barbara Kruger, Paul McCarthy and Robert Gober and be sure check out the surrounding neighborhood, **Little Tokyo**, the largest Japanese community outside of Japan *(see Neighborhoods).*

MOCA at the Pacific Design Center

8687 Melrose Ave., West Hollywood. 213-626-6222. www.moca-la.org.

The most recent addition to the MOCA family is a 3,000sq ft gallery in the compact building next to the Pacific Design Center *(see Landmarks).* Opened in 2001, it showcases changing exhibits from MOCA's permanent collection, focusing on architecture and design.

Museum of the American West★★

4700 Western Heritage Way, Griffith Park. 323-667-2000 www.autry-museum.org. Open year-round Tue–Sun 10am–5pm (Thu until 8pm). $7.50.

Formerly called the Autry Museum of Western Heritage, after its founder, the beloved "Singing Cowboy" Gene Autry (1907–1998), the museum is dedicated to preserving and presenting the story of the American West. The Autry Foundation donated the seed collection of Western art and artifacts—the number of which has grown to 78,000—and funded the construction of the Mission Revival-style building, which opened in 1988.

Seven spacious permanent galleries on the museum's main and lower levels display the collection thematically and in roughly chronological order. The **Children's Discovery Center** has a small-scale replica of an Arizona ranch house and fun things for kids to do and see.

Spirit of Community★ – Depicts the formation of a social fabric among settlers. See a diagram drawn by Wyatt Earp of the so-called 1881 "Gunfight at the OK Corral" in Tombstone, Arizona; personal firearms, and other artifacts that belonged to such famous figures as Earp, Billy the Kid, "Black Bart," and Belle Starr.

> ### Ninth U.S. Cavalry Parade Flag
> The unique 39-star flag, dating from 1889, was discovered by an officer involved with the decommissioning of Fort Sheridan, near Chicago, in the 1980s. Its maker assumed that Dakota would become the thirty-ninth state; however, Congress divided the territory in two (North and South Dakota), so a current flag at the time had to have 40 stars.

Spirit of Romance – Examines the 19C glamorization of the West. Featured are "Buffalo Bill" Cody's Burgess rifle and Annie Oakley's L.C. Smith double-barrel shotgun.

Museum of Tolerance★★

9786 W. Pico Blvd. 310-553-8403. www.museumoftolerance.org. Open Apr–Oct Mon–Thu 11:30am–6:30pm (rest of the year 5pm), Fri 11:30am–4pm, & Sun 11am–7:30pm. Closed Sat & all other Jewish and national holidays. $10.

The newest and largest multimedia exhibition at this "museum of ideas," which was dedicated in 1993, is called Finding Our Families, Finding Ourselves. It illustrates how diversity inspired noted Americans such as Dr. Maya Angelou, Billy Crystal, Carlos Santana and Joe Torre. Archival collections include artifacts from Auschwitz, personal items owned by Anne Frank, and photographs and video testimonies of Holocaust survivors.

Natural History Museum of Los Angeles County★★

900 Exposition Blvd. 213-763-3466. www.nhm.org. Open year-round Mon–Fri 9:30am–5pm, weekends 10am–5pm. Closed major holidays. $9.

The third-largest Natural History Museum in the country (after those in New York City and Washington, DC) contains more than 35 million artifacts and specimens from the fields of life sciences, earth sciences and history. Opened as the Museum of History, Science and Art in 1913, it is housed in a dignified Beaux-Arts Structure that features an elaborate marble rotunda at the eastern end.

Dueling Dinosaurs, the skeletons of a tyrannosaur and a triceratops poised for battle, delight kids. Imagine such creatures loping down the highways of LA! The museum also produces temporary special exhibits, such as LA: Light, Motion, Dreams, a look at the interplay between nature and culture in LA.

Hall of American History★ – Trace the evolution of the US from Columbus to the industrial age.

Hall of Birds★ – A 17,000sq-ft space filled with ingenious animated displays.

Hall of Gems and Minerals★ – Ogle exquisite star rubies, emeralds and sapphires, and 300 pounds of natural gold.

Times Mirror Hall of Native American Cultures★ – Visit replicas of a California Craftsman-style bungalow and a Pueblo cliff dwelling.

> **Bigger and Better**
>
> The Natural History Museum recently chose world-renowned architect Steven Holl to renovate and expand its facilities. The $100 million project is set to start in 2006, with an anticipated first-phase completion date of 2009. The new structure will be the architectural and culture corner-stone of 160-acre Exposition Park.

Everything's Coming Up Roses – Since 1928, the seven-acre sunken **Rose Garden★** has been dedicated exclusively to the cultivation of roses—nearly 20,000 specimens of more than 190 varieties. The Blooming of the Rose Festival takes place in April *(the garden is located along Exhibition Blvd., immediately east of the museum's original entrance).*

Page Museum at the La Brea Tar Pits★★ – [M¹] *refer to map on inside back cover. See Landmarks.*

Petersen Automotive Museum★★

6060 Wilshire Blvd. (at Fairfax Ave.). 323-930-2277. www.petersen.org. Open year-round Tue–Sun 10am–6pm. Closed major holidays. $10.

Thanks to massive irrigation projects, which have enabled the city to expand into the desert, and a general disdain for public transportation (that is changing, finally), LA is the quintessential car town. This museum explores the effect autos have had on the city and its people. In 1994 founding benefactors Robert and Margie Petersen donated $5 million to the Los Angeles County Natural History Museum to fund the auto museum. In 2000, the couple donated another $24.8 million.

Parked in what was formerly Ohrbach's department store are 200 restored cars, trucks and motorcycles in displays and lifelike dioramas.

First Floor – "Streetscape" takes visitors on a winding journey through 30-plus exhibits that illustrate the automobile's vital role in shaping modern-day Los Angeles.

Second Floor – Five major galleries encompass 35,000sq ft of changing exhibits and state-of-the-art displays. See hot rods in the Bruce Meyer Gallery; motorcycles in the Otis Chandler Motorcycle Gallery; and, in the Hollywood Gallery, cars that put the "motion" in motion pictures—that is, a changing array of autos owned by celebrities and used in movies and television.

Third Floor – Why does your bicycle stand upright while it's moving? How does your car's engine work? What will the car of tomorrow use for energy? At the hands-on **Discovery Center,** kids will learn the answers to these questions and more.

French Curves: The Automobile as Sculpture

French-bodied automobiles, designed according to the "streamlined moderne" aesthetic of the Art Deco school—a favorite in LA—are considered to be some of the most beautiful cars ever created. This temporary exhibit, which runs through January 24, 2005, celebrates the auto-artistry of Delahaye, Bugatti, Hispano-Suiza, and others, as rendered by Figoni et Falaschi, Saoutchik, Letourneur et Marchand, and Chapron.

Skirball Cultural Center★★

2701 N. Sepulveda Blvd. 310-440-4500. www.skirball.org. Open year-round Tue–Sat noon–5pm, Sun 11am–5pm. Closed Mon. Multilingual, docent-led tours Tue–Sun 1pm & 2:30pm. $8.

Come celebrate the Jewish American experience. This stunning architectural campus was designed by renowned Canadian architect Moshe Safdie. When its expansion is completed in 2005, it will be the largest Jewish cultural institution in North America, with a three-story multi-use hall, an amphitheater, and Noah's Park for kids. The core exhibition traces the experiences and accomplishments of the Jewish people over 4,000 years. Galleries include multimedia installations, rare artifacts, photographs, interactive computer stations and sound recordings that lead visitors on the Jewish people's journey, culminating with their history in the United States.

Southwest Museum★★

234 Museum Dr. 323-221-2164. www.southwestmuseum.org. Open year-round Tue–Sun 10am–5pm. Closed Mon & major holidays. $6.

Founded by eccentric author and activist Charles Fletcher Lummis *(see Historic Sites/Lummis House)* and opened to the public in 1914, the Southwest Museum holds one of the nation's preeminent collections of American Indian, Spanish Colonial, Latino and Western American art and artifacts.

On the first floor, the **Plains Hall** features an outstanding collection of everyday and ceremonial garments and is dominated by an 18ft Southern Cheyenne tepee. The **Southwest Hall** includes 12,000 year-old Clovis points, the earliest evidence of human life in the American Southwest. The adjoining **Basketry Study Room** displays rotating selections from the museum's 12,000-piece Native American basket collection.

Museum of Television & Radio★

465 Beverly Dr. 310-786-1000. www.mtr.org. Open year-round Wed–Sun noon–5pm. Closed Mon, Tue & major holidays. $10.

The curved façade of architect Richard Meier's transparent glass window walls invite you inside its light-filled lobby to corridors lined with media art and artifacts. The collection of American broadcasting heritage duplicates that of the MT&R in New York City. Browse, sit at individual viewing and listening consoles, don headphones or attend live radio broadcasts (such as *Car & Driver Show*), tapings, screenings, seminars and lectures.

California ScienCenter★ – *700 State Dr. See Musts for Kids.*

Hollywood Entertainment Museum★ – *7021 Hollywood Blvd., Hollywood. See Neighborhoods.*

Many of LA's landmarks—from the city's defining new icon, the Walt Disney Concert Hall, to dozens of streamlined Art Deco buildings—are clustered in the historic core of the Downtown Business District. They're particularly prevalent on and around Grand Avenue, which is reinventing itself as a cultural corridor in the tradition of the Champs Elysées in Paris and Las Ramblas in Barcelona.

Walt Disney Concert Hall★★★

111 S. Grand Ave. 323-850-5200. www.laphil.org/wdch. Audio tours ($10) offered on non-matinee days 9am–3pm; matinee days 9am–10:30am. For more information, see Performing Arts.

The curvilinear chrome-skinned lines of the Walt Disney Concert Hall, home of the Los Angeles Philharmonic, became the city's most recognizable icon even before it opened in October 2003. Architect Frank Gehry's dramatic design was immediately hailed as a symphony in steel and *the* symbol of Los Angeles. Planned as an "intimate living room for the city," it is expected to add one million downtown visitors annually. Folks come to admire its abstractionist architecture; tour the public spaces; snap pictures; linger in the shaded gardens by the mirror-finished, stainless-steel wall of the Keck Amphitheater; and gawk.

Lobby – Skylights shed natural rays on a grand staircase designed so formally clad patrons can make a true Hollywood entrance. Unique tree-shaped, wooden columns have "branches" that conceal structural steel beams and practical necessities such as conduits for electricity, lighting and air conditioning.

Auditorium – In the unique "vineyard-shaped" hall, up to 2,265 audience members can be seated around the orchestral stage and can look up to a curved-wood ceiling and ahead to the Gehry-designed **pipe organ.** The 72-stop organ has 4,200 pipes and is itself a stunning piece of contemporary art.

Edythe and Eli Broad Reception Hall – A warm cocoon of curved wood panels.

Biltmore Hotel★★

506 S. Grand Ave. 213-624-1011. www.millenniumhotels.com.

A grand hotel is the prerequisite of a great metropolis, and this 1,000-room masterpiece, built in 1923 and fashioned after a 16C Italianate palace, raised the world's opinion of Los Angeles by embracing people's imagination, much as the new Walt Disney Concert Hall does today.

Constructed at the enormous cost of $10 million, "the host of the coast" incorporates extensive brickwork, terra-cotta tile floors, extraordinary woodwork, bas-relief sculptures and tall columns topped by golden capitals in its reception halls. In 1969, the Biltmore was designated a historic and cultural monument, and in the subsequent years it has been restored and renovated to its original splendor. It is now part of the Millennium Hotel group.

Giovanni Smeraldi Ceilings – As you walk through the Galleria—the hotel's chief thoroughfare—you'll pass under a cathedral-like ceiling painted by Giovanni Smeraldi. Much like Michelangelo, he did the work lying on his back. The ceilings in the Crystal Ballroom show glimmering goddesses, cupids and mythical figures. The hotel ballroom was long *the* venue for elite events—including a number of Academy Award ceremonies.

Hotel Trivia

- It's rumored that the design of the present-day Oscar was drawn on a napkin at one of the early Academy Award events held here.

- The Biltmore Hotel claims that it has been used in more films and TV shows than any other hotel in the country. A tiny sampling: *West Wing, Providence, NYPD Blue, King Kong, Chinatown, The Pink Panther, Ocean's Eleven* and *Shopgirl*.

- The lavishly tiled indoor pool on the lower level was where Warren Beatty was pampered in *Bugsy*.

Rendezvous Court★

If there's a "must do" downtown, it's a look-see and a cup of tea in the four-story Rendezvous Court at the historic Biltmore Hotel. Step down the grand double staircase and sit in rococo opulence under a spectacular vaulted Spanish Renaissance ceiling. From 2pm to 5pm, the menu offers a proper English tea with finger sandwiches, freshly baked pastries and scones *($20.50 per person)*. Light meals, cocktails and desserts are served all day *(11:30am–10pm)*.

Bradbury Building★★

304 S. Broadway. Open year-round Mon–Fri 8am–5pm. 213-626-1893.

While the brick exterior is modest, step inside and you'll find one of the most beautiful and significant interior spaces in Los Angeles. Mining magnate Louis Bradbury originally commissioned leading local architect Sumner P. Hunt to design his headquarters building. Dissatisfied with Hunt's plans, Bradbury fired him and hired George H. Wyman, a draftsman in Hunt's firm, in his place. Bradbury didn't live to see its completion in 1893, however. Today it is occupied by the Los Angeles Police Department and other government agencies.

Interior – The splendid atrium was inspired by a description of a commercial building in Edward Bellamy's utopian novel *Looking Backward* (2000). Skylights let in natural light and air. The balconies are framed by lacelike wrought-iron railings. The open-cage elevator soars upward majestically. Wyman also threw in dashes of color: center-cut red oak on the ceilings, pink Belgium marble on the stair treads and glazed, yellow Chicago common brick and Mexican tiles on the floor. Ask the security guard for a brochure for all the details.

Eastern Columbia Building★★

849 S. Broadway.

Faced in turquoise and gold glazed terra cotta, the 13-story Art Deco landmark (1930) presents a bevy of geometric shapes, zigzags, chevrons and stylized animal and plant forms. Atop the building, you'll see a four-sided, two-story clock tower, the word "Eastern" in neon (the building was formerly the headquarters of the Eastern Outfitting Company and the Columbia Outfitting Company) and a central smokestack surrounded by four stylized flying buttresses. The two-story vestibule sports a blue-and-gold terra-cotta sunburst.

Grauman's Chinese Theatre★★ – *6925 Hollywood Blvd. See Neighborhoods/Hollywood.*

Broadway Movie Palaces

Broadway between Third & Ninth Sts.

Nickelodeons and vaudeville houses sprang up along bustling Broadway in 1910, offering live stage performances for a buck and then "live theater on film" for a nickel. By 1931 Broadway boasted the world's highest concentration of ornate movie palaces. Today nine preserved structures are used as sets for movies, TV shows and commercials. If you're in town in June, check out the LA Conservancy's Last Remaining Seats program of Wednesday-night classic films *(213-623-2489 or www.laconservancy.org)*.

Los Angeles City Hall★★

200 N. Spring St. (entrance on Main St.). 213-978-1995 (for tours). www.lacity.org/cityhall. Open year-round Mon–Fri 7:30am–5pm; hours vary on weekends.

Standing apart from the glittering skyscrapers just to the southwest, City Hall's 28-story, pyramid-topped tower remains one of downtown Los Angeles' most distinctive landmarks. It reopened in 2001 after a four-year, $300-million restoration project brought back its Art Deco splendor and shored it up against future earthquakes. Construction began in the 1920s, after the passage of a special variance allowing it to reach its full stature, and ended in 1928. Symbolically, the mortar consisted of sand from every California county and water from each of the state's 21 missions.

Interior – The tiled dome of the 135ft-wide **rotunda**★ depicts the duties of government: Public Service, Health, Trust, Art, Protection, Education and Government. The dazzling floor is composed of 46 varieties of marble cut into 4,156 inlays.

Observation Deck – The 27th-floor Bradley Room observation deck affords, on clear days, sweeping **panoramas**★★ of the Los Angeles Basin.

Pacific Design Center★★

8687 Melrose Ave. 310-657-0800. www.pacificdesigncenter.com. Open year-round Mon–Fri 9am–5pm.

Cesar Pelli, the Argentine architect, is responsible for this postmodern center for retail and art, which opened in 1975. The original building, seven stories sheathed in cobalt-blue glass, is know to locals as the Blue Whale. A hexagonal green-glass annex got the nickname "the Green Turtle." Plans are already in the works for second annex made with red glass. (What will its name be? The Red Robin? The Ladybug?) Inside the complex you'll find showrooms filled with fabric, frames, furniture and other interior-design products; the **Museum of Contemporary Art**★★ is also located here *(see Museums)*.

California Plaza★

Grand Ave. between 3rd & 4th Sts.

The 11-acre urban park replaced a historic residential neighborhood of Victorian brownstones during the urban renewal craze of the 1960s. The first tower was built in 1985. In 1992 three more buildings were completed: the 52-story second tower (the Watercourt), the Museum Tower condominium and the 17-story Hotel InterContinental (now the Omni Hotel). Watercourt Plaza features shops, restaurants and a public entertainment space that is known, today, for its **Grand Performances**, a series of free summer concerts.

Grand Central Market★

317 S. Broadway. 213-624-2378. www.grandcentralsquare.com. Open daily 9am–6pm. Closed major holidays. See Must Shop.

The city's oldest and largest open-air market sits on the ground floor of the Homer Laughlin Building (1897), which once housed an office for American architect Frank Lloyd Wright. The ground floor, originally a department store, was transformed into the market it is today in 1917. While the exterior has remained the same, the interior is now a cavernous open space, brightened with vintage neon signs. Thirty-eight multicultural merchants sell everything from farm-fresh produce and seafood to legumes and deli meats to cut flowers and take-out food. The market is a favorite of downtown employees and foot-weary visitors looking for a quick bite.

Angel's Flight

S. Hill St. between California Plaza & Grand Central Market.

This fanciful wrought-iron funicular used to be known as the "Los Angeles Incline Railway" and "The World's Shortest Railway." Beginning in 1901, the railway carried millions of passengers on Sinai and Olivet, its counterbalanced passenger cars traveling up and down 315ft between the shops of Grand Central Market and Bunker Hill, then a ritzy neighborhood of Victorian brownstones. Demolished in the 1960s (along with the rest of Bunker Hill), it was rebuilt in the 1990s and reopened in 1996. Service was again discontinued in 2001, however, after an accident killed one person and injured seven. As of press time, the future of Angel's Flight was uncertain.

Hollywood Sign★

In Griffith Park. 323-469-8311.

These nine 50ft-tall, 30ft-wide white steel letters, crookedly arranged on a grassy hillside, have become a global icon for the cockeyed dreams of Tinseltown. Erected in 1923 as an advertisement for the Hollywoodland housing development, they fell into disrepair after 1939. A SOS (Save Our Sign) civic group raised money to preserve them; finally, in 1973, the sign was declared a national monument.

The best view of the Hollywood sign is from the Griffith Observatory, but that is closed until 2005. To get a different angle, try the running track around Lake Hollywood (a reservoir near Universal Studios).

La Brea Tar Pits★

5801 Wilshire Blvd. 323-934-7243. www.tarpits.org. Museum open year-round Mon–Fri 9:30am–5pm, weekends 10am–5pm. Closed major holidays. $7. Pit viewing is free.

Lions and camels and mammoths, oh, my! It's hard to believe that smack in the middle of this metropolis, there's a bubbly black swamp that dates from the Ice Age. But it's not merely a weird geographical phenomenon, it's a rich archaeological one. Thousands of years ago, the Los Angeles basin was crowded with mammoths, bison, dire wolves, camels, and giant one-ton sloths. Unfortunately for them, many met their death here in the sticky black gunk that oozes from the La Brea Tar Pits. Fortunately for us, the tar is an amazing preservative. Millions of fossils have been excavated from the site since the first documented find in the mid-1700s, and the discoveries keep coming.

Page Museum at the La Brea Tar Pits★★ – [M¹] *refers to map on inside back cover. At the east end of Hancock Park.* Flanked by life-size replicas of extinct mammals, the museum has the largest and most diverse assemblage of extinct Ice

Age plants and animals in the world. Start with the documentary film, then proceed to the fascinating exhibits. Displays include numerous painstakingly reconstructed fossilized skeletons of such animals as dire wolves, saber-toothed cats and huge mastodons. In the Paleontology Laboratory, you can look through windows and watch ancient bones being cleaned and repaired.

What a Pit! – You can view the pits year-round, but active excavations of Pit 91 take place only in July and August. You can watch the action from a special observation deck set up at the museum next door. When strolling near the pits, wear good shoes and walk carefully, as the asphalt tends to ooze up.

Say That Again?

California has a problem with names. Many place names are derived from Spanish and include everything you need to know about the site. Take Sierra Nevada, for example. In Spanish that means Nevada Mountains. Anglicize it, as many people do, to Sierra Nevada Mountains, and you get Nevada Mountains Mountains. The same thing is true for the La Brea Tar Pits. *La brea* means "tar" in Spanish, so you're actually saying Tar Tar Pits. The city's bilingual residents must spend much of their time cringing.

Library Tower★

633 W. 5th St. between Flower St. & Grand Ave.

When I. M. Pei & Partners built this 73-story Italian granite skyscraper (1991), it was the tallest building (1,017ft) west of the Mississippi. Pei topped the building with a distinctive illuminated crown and employed a zigzag motif that pays homage to the many examples of Art Deco architecture in the immediate vicinity. An office building, it is called the Library Tower because the owners purchased air rights above the Los Angeles Central Library *(below)* directly across Fifth Street. Those funds paid for the library's restoration and expansion after it was seriously damaged by fire. Film buffs will recognize this distinctive building from scenes in the 1996 film *Independence Day*.

Los Angeles Central Library★

630 W. 5th St. (between Flower St. & Grand Ave.). 213-228-7000. www.lapl.org. Open year-round Mon–Thu 10am–8pm, Fri–Sat 10am–6pm, Sun 1–5pm. Closed major holidays.

This grand building, completed in 1926, was conceived as an allegory on the "light of learning." Its imposing tower, topped by a pyramid, echoes that of nearby City Hall. Air rights purchased by the builders of I.M. Pei tower provided the funds to restore the library when it was threatened by demolition after fire damage in 1986. The library reopened in 1993 with a sculpture garden and a new wing doubling the facility's space.

The Original Pantry

877 S. Figueroa St. at 9th St. 213-972-9279.

Blue collars and white collars mingle freely at this downtown institution, open round-the-clock since 1924 and renowned for its gargantuan portions and greased-lightning service. Downtowners can start the day with an omelette and hash browns; night owls stop by in the wee hours for steaks and chops with potatoes and slaw.

Interior – During the Great Depression, the Federal Arts Program (part of the WPA) commissioned Dean Cornwell to paint the history of Los Angeles in the library's main **rotunda**. His murals portray eras of discovery, mission building, Americanization and the founding of Los Angeles. Note the two-ton cast-bronze chandelier.

Pershing Square★

Bounded by S. Hill St., S. Olive St., W. 5th St. & W. 6th St.

This landscaped area is a vibrant gathering place in the heart of the city. It started in 1866 as a formal Spanish plaza called La Plaza Abaja; by the late 19C it was the centerpiece of a residential neighborhood and had been appropriately renamed Central Park. In 1918, "in a fit of Armistice Day fever," Central Park's name was changed again, this time to Pershing Square, in honor of the famous general. The doughboy statue in the corner—*doughboy* was the term used for American infantrymen in France during the war—dates from that period.

More recently, world-renowned architect Ricardo Legoretta redesigned the public space in 1994, and Laurie Olin, an equally celebrated landscape architect, selected the plantings. Today the Parks Department sets up an ice-skating rink in winter and holds a free concert series here in the summer.

What's What Facing Pershing Square?

- **Biltmore Hotel**★★ (1923) – *515 S. Olive St.*
- **Subway Terminal Building** (1925) – *417 Hill St.*
- **Title Guarantee and Trust Building** (1930) – *401 W. 5th St.*

Union Station★

800 N. Alameda St.

When you first glimpse the majestic white building, with its Spanish Colonial architecture and Moorish, Mission and Modern influences, you'll understand why Los Angeles Union Passenger Terminal, known simply as Union Station, is considered to be "the last of America's great rail stations"—and why it is so often used as a film location. Completed in 1939, the station brought the Southern Pacific, Atchison Topeka and Santa Fe, and Union Pacific Railroad terminals together under a single roof.

Traxx

In Union Station. 213-625-1999. Open for lunch Mon–Fri, dinner Mon–Sat. Closed Sun.
Off the main concourse you'll find Traxx, a bar/restaurant that resembles a rail dining car with its dropped ceiling and subtly curved walls. Chef-owner Tara Thomas serves contemporary American eclectic cuisine that's popular with pre-theater and post-Olvera Street crowds. Try Manila clams in Thai curry broth, crab cakes, or pan-roasted beef tenderloin with rosemary-gorgonzola crust.

As rail service declined in the 1970s and 1980s, so did the prospects of lovely Union Station, which stood empty for years. Recently Amtrak worked a bit of magic, though, drawing back some customers with its popular California coast routes (no service to Las Vegas yet, unfortunately). The city has also chipped in: Union Station is now also the hub of Metrolink, LA's commuter rail system, and Metro Rail, the newly expanded streetcar/subway network, with service to Hollywood (the Red Line) and Pasadena (Gold Line). Behind the station, the Gateway Transit Center thrums with local buses; out front you can catch a taxi.

Interior – Marble floors, leather seating, and towering vaulted ceilings beamed with fine, dark wood highlight the interior. The gracious light-filled waiting area opens to a walled outdoor patio.

Westin Bonaventure Hotel★

404 S. Figueroa St. 213-624-1000. www.westin.com.

Look familiar? These five mirrored-glass, 35-story cylindrical towers put LA on the map in 1976 as a center of post-Modern (some would say cold) architecture. Since then they've appeared in numerous futuristic films, including Ridley Scott's classic *Blade Runner* (1982). Designed by John Portman, the complex forms a city unto itself, allowing conventioneers and other business travelers to be in LA without ever having to step foot outside. (Beats traffic—perhaps.) The mall-like, six-level inner atrium is composed of several levels of shops, restaurants and meeting places.

Take a Ride – You don't have to be a guest of the hotel to take a ride on the glass-enclosed **elevators** that rise up the side of the building. They offer incredible **views★** of downtown and the Los Angeles Basin.

Bona Vista Lounge

In the Westin Bonaventure Hotel. Open daily 4pm–1am.
Every city needs a revolving rooftop cocktail lounge, and this is LA's. Perched on the 35th floor of the Bonaventure, the casual bar makes a full, 360-degree rotation every hour, letting you view the whole panorama of LA without getting out of your chair. In addition to cocktails, you can order appetizers and desserts.

Cathedral of Our Lady of the Angels

555 W. Temple St. 213-637-7000. www.olacathedral.org.

Designed by Pritzker Prize-winner Jose Rafael Moneo of Madrid, this sand-colored cathedral was completed in 2002, replacing the church destroyed in the earthquake of 1994. At 48,000sq ft, the seat of the archdiocese of Los Angeles holds 2,500 parishioners and, because it is one foot longer than St. Patrick's Cathedral in New York City, ranks as the third-largest Roman Catholic cathedral in the world.

Exterior – The 5.5-acre site is decked out with Mission-style colonnades, biblically inspired gardens, and a 150ft-tall, copper-roofed campanile with three large tolling bells.

Interior – Natural light enters through alabaster clerestory windows and illuminates John Nava's tapestries, which depict 135 saints.

Knock, knock

Church doors are said to symbolize a bridge over which parishioners may travel in their journey of faith. The Great Bronze doors on the cathedral's southeast side, designed by sculptor Robert Graham and built by some 150 artists, form a rather ingenious bridge. The immense outer doors weigh 25 tons apiece, but they open easily, rotating on steel posts with a sophisticated hydraulic system. The powerful motor can open either the solid inner doors or the hollow outer doors or, for maximum effect, the two pairs of doors in majestic sequence.

Los Angeles Times Building

202 W. 1st St. between Broadway & Spring Sts.

The *LA Times*—one of the largest newspapers in the nation—is housed in a complex that takes up an entire square block just southwest of City Hall. If you don't book a tour, take a peek at the lobby: its Art Deco central structure dates from 1935 and features a rotunda with a double mural on the ceiling. The artwork, by Hugo Balin, is aptly named *The Newspaper*. Displays include an original linotype machine, a huge revolving globe, a collection of photographs and a historical journey—via facsimile pages—of the newspaper's past issues.

Tour the Times – The *LA Times* offers free 45-minute walking tours of its facilities. One tour explores the Historic Editorial Operation; the other leads visitors through the ultramodern Olympic Printing Plant *(2000 E. 8th St.)*. Tours are held weekdays at 9:30am, 11am, & 1:30pm *(reserve by phone at least one week in advance; no walk-ins allowed; 213-237-5757).*

Unlike East Coast towns such as Boston and Philadelphia, Los Angeles isn't a place that wears its history on its sleeve. That's partly because there's not much history to wear—in 1870 the city had only 5,000 residents. Since then, the only constant has been change. Natural disasters, continual urban renewal, and ongoing sprawl challenge historians to ask themselves: What is historical? What's worth preserving? Here are a few of their answers.

El Pueblo de Los Angeles Historic Monument★

845 N. Alameda St. 213-628-1274. www.cityofla.org/elp. Open year-round daily 9am–9pm. Museums closed Thanksgiving Day & Dec 25.

You'll rarely hear the term El Pueblo ("the town") used to refer to the city's historic heart. It is locally referred to as **Olvera Street★**, after the vibrant, brick-paved pedestrian path that cuts through its central **plaza (La Placita)**, which was completed in 1825.

On September 4, 1781, 44 *pobladores* of Indian, black, Spanish, and *mestizo* ancestry founded the first farming settlement a short distance southeast of Olvera Street. In 1815 a severe flood of the nearby Los Angeles River (now barely a trickle) forced the community to relocate to higher ground. They hunkered down at the present locale in 1825.

El Pueblo Celebrates

A center of ethnic pride for LA's Latino community, El Pueblo today hosts a year-round schedule of cultural celebrations. Here's a sampling:

Blessing of the Animals *(mid-Apr)* – A traditional ceremony for domestic pets.

Cinco de Mayo *(early May)* – Commemorates Mexico's defeat of French troops in the 1862 Battle of Puebla.

Mexican Independence Day *(mid-Sept)* – Celebrates Mexico's independence from Spain in 1821.

Dia de Los Muertos *(Nov 2)* – The Day of the Dead honors those who have passed away.

Las Posadas – A Christmastime candlelit procession that recalls Mary and Joseph's journey to Bethlehem.

The first official census, in 1836, recorded 2,228 inhabitants, but as Los Angeles grew, the city's population shifted to the current downtown. In the 1920s Olvera Street was badly in need of some T.L.C. Citizen activist Christine Sterling's successful campaign to revitalize the area lasted from 1926 until her death in 1963. The area is now both the cultural home of the city's Latinos—LA's largest ethnic group—and a festive open-air marketplace, with roaming mariachi bands, puppeteers, folk dancers, and poncho merchants giving visitors a taste of life south of the border.

Avila Adobe★ – *10 E. Olvera St. Open Apr–Dec daily 9am–5pm, Jan–Mar 10am–4pm.* The oldest adobe structure in the city (1818), built by former mayor Don Francisco Avila, is now a museum furnished to show how *rancheros* lived in 1840. Across the spacious courtyard, an annex features exhibits on the Los Angeles Aqueduct *(see p 21)* and the history of El Pueblo.

Pico House★ – *Southwest corner of the plaza.* This three-story structure was considered the best hotel in Southern California when it was constructed in 1870.

Firehouse No. 1 – *Southeast corner of the plaza. Open year-round Tue–Sun 10am–3pm.* The city's first firehouse (1884) later served as a saloon, lodging house and store. It now displays 19C fire-fighting equipment.

Sepulveda House Museum (Visitor Center) – *622 N. Main St. Open year-round Mon–Sat 10am–3pm.* Mexican and Anglo influences are both evident in this 1887 Victorian. The Main Street façade is an excellent example of the local Eastlake style. Within, you can view a period kitchen and bedroom; pick up an El Pueblo self-guided walking-tour brochure; and view a free 18-minute film, *Pueblo of Promise*, about the history and the development of Los Angeles.

La Golondrina Mexican Cafe

17 Olvera St. 213-628-4349. www.lagolondrina.com. Open daily 9am–9pm (weekends until 10pm). The first Mexican restaurant in LA, La Golondrina moved to Olvera Street in 1930 and has been serving traditional Mexican food here ever since. The 150-year-old building has a cool, shaded terrace that's ideal for drinking margaritas. Arrive early for a hearty breakfast of *huevos rancheros* with chorizo. Later in the day, you can enjoy ceviche, fajitas and taquitos.

Gamble House★★

4 Westmoreland Pl., Pasadena. 626-793-3334. www.gamblehouse.org. Open year-round Thu–Sun noon–3pm. Closed major holidays. $8.

Designed by Pasadena architects Charles and Henry Greene, the rambling, redwood-shingled Gamble House was built in 1908 for David and Mary Gamble (of Procter & Gamble). With its wide overhanging eaves, broad verandas and numerous windows, it is considered one of the finest examples of architecture from the early-20C Arts and Crafts movement.

Interior – Furnishings and woodwork incorporating some 20 types of wood were conceived by the Greene brothers and executed by John and Peter Hall. Emile Lange did the stained-glass windows.

Lummis House (El Alisal)★

200 E. Ave. 43 (Exit 43 off Pasadena Fwy./Rte. 110). 323-222-0546. www.socalhistory.org. Fri–Sun noon–4pm.

Between 1898 and 1912, author, editor and activist Charles Fletcher Lummis, founder of the Southwest Museum, built this house by hand out of telephone poles and granite boulders. Why? "So it would last a thousand years," he said. Furthermore, he added, "Anyone can write a book. It takes a man to make a dovetail door." Architects Sumner Hunt and Theodore Eisen helped out on the design, which blends Mission, Pueblo and Craftsman styles and complements the natural environment. The Historical Society of Southern California currently occupies the unique structure, which is also known as El Alisal ("place of the sycamores"). Outside, a "water-wise" garden displays native and Mediterranean plants that thrive here.

Interior – Though few original furnishings remain, you can see Lummis' personal collection of Native American artifacts; a window glazed with photographic plates of Indian dances; doors and built-in furniture by Maynard Dixon; and a striking Art Nouveau fireplace.

Will Rogers State Historic Park★

1501 Will Rogers State Park Rd. (off Sunset Blvd.), Pacific Palisades. 310-454-8212. www.parks.ca.gov. Open year-round daily 8am–sunset. $5 (parking).

A rugged reminder that Los Angeles was once part of the Wild West, this 165-acre ranch belonged to America's favorite cowboy philosopher, Will Rogers (1879–1935), a man who, amazingly, used to perform dead-panned monologues on current events while doing tricks with a lasso. Rogers, who was born in Oklahoma, bought this property—plus 180 acres of surrounding land—in 1922 and entertained many Hollywood stars here. It was turned into a state park following his wife's death in 1944.

Ranch House – *Currently closed for renovation; scheduled to reopen in late 2004.* As Rogers' fame grew, so did his house, which began as a weekend retreat and now encompasses 31 rooms. Today it remains largely as it was in Rogers' day. A porch swing hangs in the center of the living room, which also holds a collection of Native American rugs and baskets.

Polo Fields – *Matches held May–Sept Sat 2pm–5pm, Sun 10am–2pm.* In a departure from rodeo tradition, Rogers built a polo field for fellow players Spencer Tracy, Robert Montgomery and Walt Disney.

Hiking Trails – Venture out to Inspiration Point for fabulous **views** of the sea and the Santa Monica Mountains.

Barnsdall Art Park

4800 Hollywood Blvd. 323-644-6269. Park open year-round daily 7am–midnight. Walking tours ($5) Wed–Sun 12:30–3:30 (reservations necessary on weekdays).

In the late 1910s, oil heiress and arts patron Aline Barnsdall bought a 36-acre estate and, with Frank Lloyd Wright, developed plans for an arts complex. The project was only partially completed at the time of Barnsdall's death in 1927, but the vision lives on in the 11-acre park's architecture and cultural programs.

Hollyhock House★★ – *Closed for renovation as of mid-2004. Call for updates.* This was the first Frank Lloyd Wright building in Los Angeles. Hollyhocks—Barnsdall's favorite flower—dominate both the interior and exterior ornamentation.

Patrick's Roadhouse

106 Entrada Dr., Santa Monica. 310-459-4544. www.patricksroadhouse.com.

You can't miss the green-shamrock-studded building facing the beach on the Pacific Coast Highway. Bikers, beach bums, and celebs come here for the waffles, pancakes, home-style soups and sandwiches, and creative dinner fare like chicken chipotle. There's live music on Saturday nights.

Parks and Gardens

Hemmed in as it is between the mountains and the sea, LA has quite a lot to offer nature lovers and outdoorsy types. Chaparral and live oak cling to its steep, desolate peaks, while roses and other blooms are pampered in a number of formal gardens.

Griffith Park★★

Entrances located on Los Feliz Blvd., accessible from the Ventura Fwy. (Rte. 134), and from the Golden State Fwy. (I-5). 323-913-4688. www.griffithpark.org. Open year-round daily 6am–10pm.

The largest urban park in the country is a vast, surprisingly rugged swatch of forest, mountains and canyons just a stone's throw from Hollywood. It's a favorite spot for athletic Angelenos who want to run, cycle or Rollerblade without donning a bikini.

It originated as a generous Christmas present. In 1882 Welsh immigrant Colonel Griffith J. Griffith (yes, that is his name!) bought just over 4,000 acres of the former Spanish land grant Rancho Los Feliz. Then, on December 16, 1896, Griffith, who made his fortune in the granite-mining business, donated 3,015 acres of the ranch to the city for public use. "Give Nature a chance to do her work," he observed in 1912, "and Nature will give every person a greater opportunity in health, strength, and mental power." Additional acquisitions followed until the park reached its current size, 4,103 acres, in the 1960s.

What's What in Griffith Park

Los Angeles Zoo & Botanical Gardens★★ – *5333 Zoo Dr. See Musts for Kids.*

Museum of the American West★★ – *4700 Western Heritage Way. See Museums.*

Hollywood Sign★ – *See Landmarks.*

Griffith Observatory – *Closed for expansion until late 2005. 2800 E. Observatory Rd. 323-664-1181. www.griffithobs.org.* During the renovation of this three-domed Art Deco observatory (1935), a modest program of planetarium shows and astronomy exhibits is being offered at the **Griffith Observatory Satellite** *(4800 Western Heritage Way, next to the Western Heritage Museum).*

Greek Theatre – *2700 N. Vermont Ave. See Performing Arts.*

Hoofing It

With 53mi of hiking trails and 43mi of bridle paths, Griffith Park can be a bit overwhelming to the uninitiated. If you're on foot, let a local be your guide. Sierra Club members conduct regular hikes in the park *(213-387-4287; www.angeles.sierraclub.org).* Another great way to explore is on horseback. Saddle up for a one-hour guided trail ride at the Los Angeles Equestrian Center *(818-840-8401; open daily 7:30am–4:30pm; $20).*

Huntington Botanical Gardens★★

1151 Oxford Rd., San Marino. 626-405-2141. www.huntington.org. Open year-round Sept–May Tue–Fri noon–4:30pm, weekends 10:30am–4:30pm. Rest of the year Tue–Sun 10:30am–4:30pm. $10.

Towering palm forests, milky camellias, bristling cacti, lazy lily pads, sweeping views—this rollicking, 150-acre garden rivals the art next door for its color, texture and brilliance.

Henry Edwards Huntington (1850–1927), nephew of Central Pacific Railroad owner Collis P. Huntington, made a name for himself in Los Angeles by consolidating and expanding the city's streetcar system, the Pacific Electric Railway. In 1902 he bought the rugged working ranch known as San Marino, and in 1904 he hired landscape gardener William Hertrich to begin cultivating the grounds. Forty-five years later, Hertrich retired at the age of 70, having helped to create a masterpiece.

Today, about 15,000 species and cultivars are displayed in 15 thematic groupings. The rose and camellia gardens, both without peer, feature more than 1,400 varieties of their respective species. Elsewhere you'll find Australian plants, jungle and subtropical species, herbs and English plants mentioned in Shakespeare's plays. The romantic Temple of Love was added by Huntington's wife, Arabella, a diehard francophile.

Japanese Garden★ – The temple bell, the gracefully arched moon bridge and reflecting ponds, the stone lanterns and pagodas create a tranquil aura here. A Zen garden of raked gravel and rocks and a collection of bonsai trees is also on view. Follow the winding path downhill through a wooded setting of Japanese cedars, bamboo groves and Asian shrubs.

Desert Garden – The gently rolling terrain of this 12-acre oasis presents one of the world's largest outdoor collections of mature cacti and succulents, with more than 5,000 species.

Rose Garden Tea Room

626-683-8131. Open year-round Tue–Fri noon–4:30pm, weekends 10:45am–4:30pm (last seating at 3:30pm). Reservations required. $15 per person.

Imagine sipping tea and nibbling finger sandwiches and miniature pastries while looking out over a glorious, three-acre rose garden. The Rose Garden Tea Room is located in a building that Mr. Huntington had constructed for his private bowling alley. Now there's an elegant buffet (you can return as many times as you like), tables set with floral linens and china service, and limitless refills of tea and scones. (A more casual, family-friendly cafeteria is in the same building.)

Los Angeles County Arboretum and Botanic Garden★★

301 North Baldwin Ave. at I-210, Arcadia. 626-821-3222. www.arboretum.org. Open year-round daily 9am–4:30pm. Closed Dec 25. $6.

Pressed against the majestic background of the San Gabriel Mountains, the 127-acre site has a world-spanning plant collection and a trio of 19C structures. The land originally lay at the heart of the 13,319-acre Rancho Santa Anita. Mining millionaire and high-roller Elias Jackson "Lucky" Baldwin purchased it in 1875. His daughter, the aptly named Anita, sold the property to *LA Times* owner Harry Chandler in 1936. Chandler proceeded to show off its spring-fed lake, still the centerpiece of the grounds, in a succession of Hollywood films, starting with *The Road to Singapore* (1939). In 1947 he sold it the county for use as an arboretum.

Today 30,000 plants of more than 7,000 species are rooted on this spectacular site. Highlights include 150 of the 500 known species of eucalyptus (one of the largest collections outside Australia) and 2,299 species of orchids (one of the largest collections in the US). A flock of iridescent peacocks like to strut their stuff for the resident peahens—and for visitors.

Santa Anita Park

285 W. Huntington Dr, Arcadia. 626-574-7223. www.santaanita.com. Open late Dec–mid-Apr Wed–Sun. $5 and up. Seabiscuit won the 1940 Santa Anita Handicap at this Art Deco thoroughbred racetrack, and a life-size bronze statue, sculpted by Ted Wheeler, celebrates the victory. During World War II, the 320-acre site was used by the US government as a Japanese-American assembly center and later as US Army Camp Santa Anita. Since 2000 the park's future has been uncertain: preservationists hope that its landmark status will protect it from developers who want to turn it into a Wild West-themed entertainment center.

Queen Anne Cottage – If you think the marble-terraced cottage looks familiar, here's a hint: "Da plane, da plane!" Yup, it was none other than Ricardo Montalban's pad in the TV show *Fantasy Island*. One of several period buildings on the property, the 1885 Victorian is thought to have been a honeymoon gift from Lucky to his fourth wife, 16-year-old Lillie Bennett. Lillie's father, architect Albert A. Bennett, designed the cottage, but the honeymooners apparently never enjoyed its beauty. Lillie and Lucky separated before it was completed.

Descanso Gardens★

1418 Descanso Dr., La Cañada. 818-949-4200. www.descansogardens.org. Open year-round daily 9am–5pm. Closed Dec 25. $6.

Although descanso is derived from the Spanish verb "to rest," there's plenty you'll want to explore at this 160-acre horticultural sanctuary nestled in a hollow of the San Rafael Hills (about a 20-minute drive from downtown LA).

In 1937 E. Manchester Boddy, publisher of LA's *Daily News*, purchased this land—originally part of a ranch deeded to the Verdugo family—for his estate. First he built a 22-room mansion on a hill overlooking the site. An avid horti-culturalist, he recognized the setting's 35-acre grove of gnarled California live oaks as an ideal environment for growing camellias. His first planting, in 1941, gradually bloomed into a major operation, with 100,000 camellias in more than 600 varieties. As he expanded, he also added roses, lilacs and other flowering plants. Boddy sold the estate to Los Angeles County in 1953.

Camellia Forest★ – In bloom September to April, these milky-blossomed bushes—which ordinarily max out at 8ft—grow up to 35ft tall here, forming dense, cool groves of greenery that tower over crisscrossing footpaths.

International Rosarium – The five-acre retreat boasts 5,000 antique and modern roses in landscape vignettes. They bloom in May.

Virginia Robinson Gardens★

1008 Elden Way, Beverly Hills. 310-276-5367. http://parks.co.la.ca.us/virginia_gardens.html. Visit by guided tour only (reservations required) year-round Tue–Thu 10am & 1pm, Fri 10am. $7.

Call them pioneers. When the Robinsons built their extravagant, Mediterranean-style villa here in 1911, they had no idea who their neighbors would be—it was the first residential lot sold in Beverly Hills. Soon the sumptuous estate became a gathering point for the rich and famous. Mrs. Robinson retired from playing tennis at the age of 85, after a match with Charlie Chaplin, but she continued to entertain right up until her death just weeks before her 100th birthday. She bequeathed the estate to Los Angeles County, which opened it to the public in 1982.

Gardens – The villa is surrounded by English and terraced Mediterranean gardens, including 50 varieties of camellias.

Palm Forest – The two acres of king palms represent the largest such stand outside of Australia.

Will Rogers State Historic Park★ – *1501 Will Rogers State Park Rd. See Historic Sites.*

Barnsdall Art Park – *4800 Hollywood Blvd. See Historic Sites.*

In a town whose stock-in-trade is make-believe, you can bet that there's no lack of fun ways to spend your time. Why, half the fun is just being in LA, where you could run into your favorite celebrity around any corner. Ride a bike, take a tour, catch a game, or just go star-gazing. In LA, it's all in the name of fun.

Go for a Drink at Beverly Hills Hotel★

9641 Sunset Blvd., Beverly Hills. 310-276-2251 or 800-283-8885. www.beverlyhillshotel.com.

Whether you prefer mimosas in the morning or daiquiris at dusk, you can enjoy your favorite drink in luxury at the Beverly Hills Hotel. Here, you can soak in the rays at the **Pool Cabana Café** or wind down in opulence at the famed **Polo Lounge.** Don't be surprised if you happen to spot your favorite star while you're there—both the hotel and the lounge have been celebrity haunts for almost a century *(see Landmarks).*

Find a Glorious Sunset

There's something special about looking west as the sun sets over the Pacific, and with 81mi of coastline from Long Beach to Malibu, the Los Angeles area can provide some great viewpoints. For the best views, head to piers, parks and promenades along the ocean. If you're looking for a more refined experience, try dining at an oceanfront restaurant *(see Must Eat).*

You'll love the view from the pier in Santa Monica; look north and west to see the dramatic curve of Malibu and the high ridge of the Pacific Palisades. As the sun slips beyond the horizon, marvel at the beauty of the Strand's long stretch of sand and the beach walkers silhouetted against the darkening sky.

Go Star Gazing

The most natural way to see celebrities is to shop on **Rodeo Drive★★★** *(see Must Shop)*, eat at trendy restaurants *(see Must Eat)*, and stay at chic hotels *(see Must Stays)*. You aren't guaranteed a celebrity sighting, but you won't feel awkward if you do meet one.

If you've always wondered what your favorite celeb lives, you'll be happy to know that an entire tourism sector exists to take the curious past the homes of the rich and famous in Beverly Hills. You can find maps and tours on practically every corner, or you can plan your trip from home using Web sites like *www.seeingstars.com.* It's fine for you to drive by the stars' estates on your own, but please keep in mind that the homes are private and trespassing is illegal.

If you want to join a tour, here are a few to get you started:

Starline Tours – *Depart from Grauman's Chinese Theatre, 6925 Hollywood Blvd. 800-959-3131. www.starlinetours.com. $32.*

Hollywood Fantasy Tours – *Depart from 6231 Hollywood Blvd. (Hollywood & Vine). 323-469-8184 or 800-782-7287. www.hollywoodfantasytours.com.*

Hollywood Tours – *Depart from 7095 Hollywood Blvd., #705 (hotel pick-up available). 800-789-9575. www.hollywoodtours.us. Advance reservations required. $37.*

Take A Bike Ride

If your legs and lungs work together over long distances, try out one of LA's many bike paths. The **Los Angeles County Bicycle Coalition** *(213-629-2142; www.labikecoalition. com),* a cycling advocacy organization, features information about cycling safety and regulations, tips for enjoying a ride at any skill level, and links to trail maps and other cycling organizations.

Once you've gained a feel for the cycling environment in the city and its surroundings, you'll need to find a bike. Rentals are available in bike shops in many of LA's neighborhoods; check out the listings provided by **The Full Cycle** *(www.thefullcycle.com).* Both LA and its surroundings have miles of paths available to cyclists. If you're uncomfortable riding when cars are present, look for **Level One** paths, which are completely isolated from traffic.

Need Directions?

Here are some Web sites where you can find maps of the LA area to help you plan your biking route:

www.laparks.org – Offers maps of LA city bicycle routes and a complete list of cycling rules and regulations.

www.labikepaths.com – Look for maps of cycling trails throughout LA County here.

www.bikemetro.com – If you're feeling adventurous, use this site to plan your own cycling itinerary.

http://pen.ci.santa-monica.ca.us/gis/map_catalog/csm_map_catalog/bikemap.jpg – Provides a simple map of Santa Monica paths.

Take a Cruise

Harbor Breeze Cruises, 100 Aquarium Way, Dock #2, Long Beach. 25mi south of downtown LA via I-710 South to the Shoreline Dr. exit. From W. Shoreline Dr., turn right onto Aquarium Way. 562-432-4900. www.lasightseeingcruises.com. Prices vary.

No matter when you visit LA, you can board a ship and explore the area by sea. Harbor Breeze Cruises offers a variety of excursions year-round, ranging from a sail around the harbor, which points out LA's most interesting sights from a vantage point just off the coast, to a dolphin and sea life cruise, which transports you to the Palos Verdes Peninsula for a look at local marine life in its natural environment.

Whale-Watching Cruises – If you're in LA between the end of December and the beginning of April, don't miss going on a whale-watching cruise. Each year, gray whales migrate from the frigid waters of Alaska to the warmer waters off Baja, California, to mate and bear their calves, providing passengers with an opportunity to see these graceful creatures en route.

Catch a Game at the Rose Bowl★

15mi northeast of Los Angeles, via Rte. 2 North to Foothill Freeway (US-210) East; exit at Arroyo/Windsor and follow signs. 1001 Rose Bowl Dr., off Linda Vista Ave. in Pasadena. 626-577-3100. www.rosebowlstadium.com.

Located in Pasadena's 61-acre **Brookside Park,** the renowned Rose Bowl lies in a gorge called the Arroyo Seco, which was carved by streams long ago. Built in 1922, the Rose Bowl stadium seats 92,542. College football fans will enjoy watching the UCLA Bruins play here. If you're in town on New Year's Day, make it a point to get tickets to the annual Rose Bowl Game.

Rose Bowl Parade

Pasadena's most anticipated event—the annual Tournament of Roses Parade—takes place on New Year's Day. For two hours, a line of flower-bedecked floats, marching bands and equestrian units makes its way along a five-and-a-half mile route. Starting

at the corner of Ellis Street and Orange Grove Boulevard, the parade moves slowly north on Orange Grove, then turns east onto Colorado Boulevard, where the majority of the parade takes place. It all ends at Sierra Madre and Villa Street. Be sure to wave to the Rose Queen and her "royal" court.

For information: 626-449-7673 or www.tournamentofroses.com.

Be In A Movie

www.beinamovie.com.

Here's your chance to be a movie star . . . well, an extra, anyway. You won't make any money, but if you happen to be in town when a film shoot needs an unpaid extra for a day, you might get to appear in the background of a major feature film.

Tour Mulholland Drive★

Mulholland Dr. starts at Cahuenga Blvd., less than 1mi north of the Hollywood Bowl and meanders 20mi west to Calabasas; Mulholland picks up again at Mulholland Hwy. and continues 20mi west to Hwy. 1, near the LA/Ventura line.

Named for William Mulholland, engineer of the LA Aqueduct *(see p 21)*, Mulholland Drive is one of LA's most magnificent roads. As you navigate its gentle curves, you'll travel along the crest of the Santa Monica Mountains, overlooking the Los Angeles Basin and the San Fernando Valley below. The **views**★★ of the surrounding terrain are sure to amaze you, as are the luxurious homes you'll pass along the way. Bring extra film to capture vistas of both the city and its rugged surroundings from the **Hollywood Bowl Overlook** on the eastern side of the drive *(7036 Mulholland Dr., in Hollywood)*. If you rent an SUV, you can enjoy an off-road adventure along Mulholland's western end, which is largely unpaved between I-405 and Topanga Canyon Road.

Runyon Canyon Park

0.7mi north of Hollywood Bowl Overlook (Mulholland Dr.). Other entrances on Fuller Ave. & on Vista St. www.runyon-canyon.com.

Along the eastern part of Mulholland Drive, undeveloped Runyon Canyon Park is one of Hollywood's treasures. The canyon, which begins just above Franklin Avenue (at Fuller Ave.) and ends at Mulholland Drive, was named for former owner Carman Runyon, a retired businessman from the East. Residents in the neighborhood fought development of the site, and it became a park in 1984. Runyon Canyon attracts locals who want to enjoy a run, take a hike, or walk their dogs away from the city's bustle.

L os Angeles is not all glitz and glamour—don't forget that make-believe is a way of life here. In a metropolitan area where Disneyland was born and where an entire industry revolves around planning children's birthday parties, kids will find no lack of fun things to do.

Disneyland Resort★★★

25mi southeast of LA via I-5 South. See Excursions.

Universal Studios Hollywood★★★

100 Universal City Plaza, Universal City. See Studios.

Exposition Park★★

Bounded by S. Figueroa St., Vermont Ave. and Exposition & Martin Luther King Blvds.

LA's first cultural complex started life as an agricultural park hosting livestock shows, county fairs and horse racing. Today you'll find a treasure trove of activities within its 160 acres.

Natural History Museum of Los Angeles County★★

900 Exposition Blvd. 213-763-3466. www.nhm.org. Open Mon–Fri 9:30am–5pm, weekends 10am–5pm. Closed major holidays. $9.

The National History Museum caters to kids with hands-on activities, live reptile and fish exhibits, and a fantastic dinosaur collection that includes one

of the best T-rex skulls ever discovered. Kids will be amazed by the eerie Megamouth shark, one of only three examples on display in the world. If you're feeling brave, take your kids to the **Insect Zoo,** where they can learn about tarantulas, scorpions, centipedes and other creepy-crawlies. Kids are allowed to touch almost all the exhibits at the museum's **Discovery Center.**

California ScienCenter★

700 State Dr. 323-724-3623. www.casciencectr.org. Open daily 10am–5pm. Closed Jan 1, Thanksgiving Day & Dec 25.

With exhibits specially designed to appeal to children and a mission statement that emphasizes education, the California ScienCenter creates so much fun for kids that they hardly realize they're learning. With its broad selection of permanent exhibits, specializing in topics as varied as creativity, biology and space travel, the museum even has a thing or two to teach parents. Favorites include the **Air and Space Gallery,** where planes seem about to crash, and the **IMAX Theater,** which brings its audience into the movie.

Long Beach Aquarium of the Pacific★★

100 Aquarium Way, Long Beach. See Beach Communities.

Los Angeles Zoo & Botanical Gardens★★

5333 Zoo Dr., Griffith Park. 323-644-4200. www.lazoo.org. Open daily 10am–5pm (Jun–Aug until 6pm). Closed Dec 25. $9.

You can probably recognize a rhino, but can you point out a bongo, a yellow-footed rock wallaby or a giant eland? And what about a gerenuk or an emperor tamarin? You'll find them all at the Los Angeles Zoo, set on 113 lush acres in Griffith Park. The zoo's acclaimed collection of animals includes more than 1,200 birds, mammals, amphibians and reptiles from around the world. Of the 400 species housed here, about 70 represent rare and endangered species that the zoo has worked long and hard to save.

The zoo is constantly expanding; the new golden monkey exhibit is slated to open in 2004. Check at the entrance for a schedule of bird shows and animal-feeding sessions.

Adventure Island – Here you'll find animals from the American Southwest, including farm animals in the Hacienda; there's also an animal nursery, a children's theater and an assortment of games for youngsters.

Chimpanzees of Mahale Mountains – Part of the zoo's new Great Ape Forest, this exhibit is named for a group of wild chimps in Tanzania, Africa. You can watch the chimpanzees frolic in their open-air penthouse through large glass windows.

Museum of the American West★★

4700 Western Heritage Way, Griffith Park. See Museums.

Summer Sounds

Are the kids getting bored with all your trips to museums and shops? Why not plan an outing just for them? If you're in town during July or August, head to the Hollywood Bowl *(see Performing Arts)* for Summer Sounds, a festival of music just for kids. Concerts explore musical themes from all over the globe. There are storytelling and singing sessions, and hands-on crafts for younger children; olders can participate in art classes led by professional artists. For more information, contact the LA Philharmonic Education Department *(213-972-0704)* or check out the Hollywood Bowl's Web site *(www.hollywoodbowl.com)*.

Santa Monica Pier★★

Ocean Ave. at Colorado Blvd. 310-458-8900. www.santamonicapier.org.
See Beach Communities.

There's fun for the whole family at this wildly popular 1,000ft pier over Santa Monica Bay. Let the kids invade the arcade, go on amusement park rides and buy souvenirs, while you take in the **views**★. Preservationists began a restoration of this National Historic Landmark in the 1980s; the 1916 Hippodrome building, which houses the carousel and a Wurlitzer organ, was the first project to be completed.

Carousel★ – *350 Santa Monica Pier. 310-394-8042. www.santamonicapier.org. Open Mon–Thu 11am–5pm; Fri–Sun 11am–7pm. Closed Tue & Wed Jan–mid-Mar.* Dating back to 1916, this Charles Looff carousel with its beautiful hand-painted horses, is sure to delight kids of all ages.

Pacific Park – *380 Santa Monica Pier. 310-260-8744. www.pacpark.com. Call for hours. Unlimited ride access $19.95 for guests over 42 inches in height; $10.95 for guests under 42 inches in height; individual ride tickets available.* At the end of the Santa Monica Pier, Pacific Park features a solar-powered Ferris wheel, a steel roller coaster and myriad rides for younger kids. New attractions include Inkie's Scrambler, which makes 11 revolutions per minute; Pacific Plunge, lifting riders nine stories above Santa Monica Bay; and Pirates Pier Mini Golf.

Playland Arcade – *350 Santa Monica Pier. 310-451-5133. www.playlandarcade.com. Open May–Aug Sun–Thu 9am–12am, Fri & Sat 9am–2am. Rest of the year Sun–Thu 10am–12am, Fri & Sat 10am–2am.* This gigantic arcade features more than 200 games. Tots can try out the the mini carousel, while teens play Dance Dance Revolution, and parents reminisce with Pac Man and pinball.

Santa Monica Pier Aquarium – *1600 Ocean Front Walk. 310-393-6149. www.healthebay.org/smpa. Open year-round Tue–Fri 2pm–5pm, weekends 12:30pm–5pm. $1.* Located on the beach level below the carousel, hands-on displays, exhibits swimming with fish, and touch tanks filled with sea creatures provide a unique view into the world of marine science. Now a community program run by Heal the Bay, the aquarium was formerly the UCLA Ocean Discovery Center.

The Children's Nature Institute

1440 Harvard St., Santa Monica. 310-998-1151. www.childrensnatureinstitute.org. Daily nature walks at 10am. $7 donation per family recommended.

Come introduce the children (newborns to age 8) to nature on docent-led tours through 85 sites in LA and Ventura counties, ranging from beaches to mountains. Bring water and a snack, and meet for lizard-watching, flower-smelling, or meandering, plus sing-alongs and activities. Guides provide a wealth of information about the plants and animals you'll see along the way.

Coldwater Canyon Park

12601 Mulholland Dr. Beverly Hills. 818-753-4600. www.treepeople.org. Open year-round daily sunrise–sunset.

Set in Coldwater Canyon, on the valley side past Mulholland Drive, 44-acre Coldwater Canyon Park is the headquarters for TreePeople, a "green" group dedicated to raising local awareness about the LA environment. The group also sponsors a range of eco-tours, full-moon hikes, tree tours and a variety of children's programs at Coldwater Canyon Park. The park is a fabulous place to take the kids for a walk amid the oaks and walnut trees; while you're there, try to catch one of the kid's tales events at the 99-seat **S. Mark Taper Foundation Amphitheatre.** Look for Seedling News, the park's calendar of events, at the trailhead near the tree nursery, or call for information.

Sunset Ranch Hollywood Stables

3400 N. Beachwood Dr. 323-469-5450. www.sunsetranchhollywood.com. Open daily 9am–5pm. $20/hr, $15/hr for each additional hour. Ages 7 and up.

'Tweens and teens will love riding off into the sunset and through the 43mi of bridle paths that thread Griffith Park. On a clear day, you can see the Pacific Ocean as you ride through the Hollywood Hills. Every Friday night at 5pm, weather permitting, guides take a group of riders over the hills to the other side of the park, where they have dinner at a Mexican restaurant, and then ride back after dark. The whole excursion takes about five hours and costs $40 a person. It's first-come, first-served, so be sure to get to the ranch early.

Must Go: Performing Arts

So many performances, so little time. Would you expect anything less from the world capital of entertainment? From spirit-lifting concerts to heart-wrenching dramas, LA really knows how to put on a show. Make sure you're not last in line!

Walt Disney Concert Hall★★★

111 S. Grand Ave. 323-850-5200. www.laphil.org/wdch. See Landmarks.

Designed by avant-garde architect Frank Gehry, Walt Disney Concert Hall became *the* symbol of Los Angeles even before it opened in October 2003. Gehry's abstract design is now the crown jewel of the performing-arts complex on Grand Avenue, and the new 2,265-seat home of the **Los Angeles Philharmonic**.

REDCAT (Roy and Edna Disney Cal Arts Theatre) – *In the Walt Disney Concert Hall. 213-237-2800. www.redcatweb.org.* This small (250-seat) theater in the Disney Concert Hall was designed to showcase the work of artists based in the LA community. Its inaugural season featured electronic-music composer Morton Subotnick, post-minimalist composer Gavin Bryers, and a festival of Persian and Indian music.

Music Center of Los Angeles County

135 N. Grand Ave. 213-972-7211. www.musiccenter.org.

The heart of LA's performing-arts scene, the Music Center consists of an elegant group of three white-marble structures resting on a 10-acre elevated plaza downtown. In 2003 the Walt Disney Concert Hall added a fourth venue to the complex; it's linked to the rest of the center across First Street.

The Music Center opened to great acclaim with a performance of the LA Philharmonic Orchestra in the 3,197-seat Dorothy Chandler Pavilion in 1964. Since then it has added two more theaters, the Ahmanson and the Mark Taper Forum to its ranks.

Dorothy Chandler Pavilion★ – *135 N. Grand Ave. 213-972-8001 www.losangelesopera.com.* As it approaches its 20th anniversary, the Dorothy Chandler Pavilion, home of the **Los Angeles Opera**, continues to expand under the direction of famous tenor Placido Domingo.

Ahmanson Theatre – *135 N. Grand Ave. 213-972-7211. www.ahmansontheatre.com.* The Ahmanson stages major Broadway musicals, wide-appeal dramas, comedies and revivals. *Phantom of the Opera* played here, as did Baz Luhrmann's production of Puccini's *La Boheme*. The venue can accommodate more than 2,000 people.

Mark Taper Forum – *135 N. Grand Ave. 213-972-7211 www.ahmansontheatre.com.* Sister theater to the Ahmanson, the award-winning 752-seat Mark Taper Forum specializes in cutting-edge plays and musicals.

Hollywood Bowl★★

2301 N. Highland Ave., Hollywood. 323-850-2000. www.hollywoodbowl.com.
Grounds open year-round daily dawn to dusk. Summer performance season runs from
late June to late Sept.

Attending a concert at the Bowl has long been a favorite diversion for Angelenos. Opened in 1922, the Hollywood Bowl is the summer home of the LA
Philharmonic and the Hollywood Bowl Orchestra (the venue's resident en-
semble). Frank Sinatra, The Beatles, Igor Stravinsky, Ella Fitzgerald and Luciano
Pavarotti have all played the Bowl. With top-drawer performances, seats for
18,000, and reasonable ticket prices, it's no wonder that the Bowl packs in
record-breaking crowds, year after year. Although eating at the amphitheater
was once discouraged, picnicking before a concert has now become a much-
loved Los Angeles tradition here—patrons who favor formality may even drag
out their silver candelabras.

The Hollywood Bowl is one of the world's largest natural amphitheaters, occupying a broad hollow in the Santa Monica Mountains surrounded by 120
acres of greenery. Over time, the development of Beverly Hills and the ever-
increasing crowds have posed a constant challenge to the Bowl's acoustics. To
remedy the problem, the orchestral shell has been designed and redesigned
more than five times over the past 75 years, with the most recent renovations
adding state-of-the-art lighting and sound technology in 2004. More than just
a music venue, the Bowl has hosted fireworks displays, high school commence-
ment exercises and even an occasional wedding. If you're in LA during the
summer months, be sure to schedule a night out at the Hollywood Bowl.

Gourmet Dining at the Hollywood Bowl

The Patina Group, 323-850-1885. www.patinagroup.com.

Don't worry about preparing a picnic when you visit the Hollywood Bowl. Thanks to
the Patina Group, under the direction of master chef and restaurateur Joachim Splichal
and his wife, Christine, you can get a gourmet dinner at the Bowl. Box-seat patrons can
opt to have their meal delivered to their seats as long as they've placed their order at
least a day in advance. If you want to be more spontaneous, you can buy a pre-pack-
aged gourmet dinner at **Stacatto's,** create your own basket at **The Marketplace**, or
enjoy a three-course prix-fixe menu *($27)* at the **Rooftop Grill** *(reservations: 323-850-
1885).* Finally, even the culinary-challenged can enjoy a great picnic at the Bowl.

Pantages Theatre★

6233 Hollywood Blvd. 323-468-1770. www.broadwayla.org.

Vaudeville impresario Alexander Pantages opened the theater in 1930 as the first Art Deco movie palace in the US; from 1949 to 1959 it hosted the Academy Awards. Currently a venue for musicals and dance productions, the Pantages underwent a $10-million renovation in 2000 to restore the theater to its original glory— just in time to produce *The Lion King*. Big Broadway hits, ranging from *Oklahoma* and *The King and I* to *Mamma Mia* and *Moving Out*, take the stage year-round.

Interior – From its understated concrete and black-marble exterior, you'd never guess what opulence lies inside. Marble and plaster walls adorn the lobby, which is covered by a brightly lit domed ceiling. Within the 2,700-seat auditorium, the three-dimensional ceiling seems almost sculptural with its bronze scroll patterns, silver rays and heavy gold frames that surround the theater's massive original chandelier.

Wiltern Theatre★

3790 Wilshire Blvd. Information: 213-388-1400. Box office: 213-380-5005. www.wiltern.com.

This former Warner cinema is the centerpiece of the eye-catching, turquoise terra-cotta **Pellissier Building** (1931), a 12-story Art Deco tower with two commercial wings. The Wiltern debuted its first movie in 1931; in more recent years, this Art Deco landmark has become a concert venue, hosting music greats like singer Bob Dylan, rockers the Rolling Stones and David Bowie, as well as comedians Eddie Izzard, Margaret Cho and Ellen Degeneres.

The fanciful interior, with its elaborate sunburst ceiling, was once described by its designer, Anthony B. Heinsbergen, as a "steaming jungle" of pinks, purples and oranges. The Wiltern's most recent renovation added a five-tiered floor in the orchestra section and created seating for 2,300 people.

Get Your Tickets Here
Try these ticket outlets for productions in LA:

Theatre L.A. *(213-614-0556, ext. 810; www.theatrela.org)* handles tickets to stage performances and offers half-price tickets.

Ticketmaster – *(213-480-3232; www.ticketmaster.com)* sells tickets for concerts, sporting events and theater.

Kodak Theatre

6801 Hollywood Blvd. at Highland Ave., Hollywood. Information: 323-308-6300. Box office: 323-308-6363. www.kodaktheatre.com.

You can almost hear the words ". . . and the winner is. . ." as you walk down the aisle here. Custom-designed for live TV broadcasts, the Kodak Theatre opened in 2001 as the new high-tech home of the Academy Awards. When it's not hosting the awards ceremony, the Kodak brings concerts musicals, ballet and special events to its stage.

Behind the Scenes

Want to know where your favorite movie star sat during the Academy Awards this year? Take a tour of the Kodak Theatre and find out. You'll be able to sneak a peek at venue's state-of-the-art technology as well.

Tours are held year-round daily 10:30am–2:30pm; $15. Call 323-308-6363. Tickets can be purchased up to 7 days in advance at the theater's box office (open Mon–Sat 10am–6pm, Sun 10am–2:30pm).

Greek Theatre

2700 N. Vermont Ave., in Griffith Park. 323-665-1927. www.greektheatrela.com. Season: May–Oct.

Nestled in Griffith Park, the legendary Greek Theatre is the three-time winner of the prestigious Pollstar Award for the nation's Best Small Outdoor Venue. The 6,162-seat facility celebrated its 75th anniversary with a multimillion-dollar renovation in the spring of 2004. From Paul Simon to the Russian National Ballet to Sir Paul McCartney, you'll find a wide range of big-name performers here, bringing LA some of its best entertainment under the stars.

Pasadena Playhouse

39 S. El Molino Ave., Pasadena. Box office: 626-356-7529. www.pasadenaplayhouse.org.

Known as "Hollywood's talent factory" during the 1930s, 40s and 50s, the Pasadena Playhouse helped launch the careers of countless stars, including Dustin Hoffman and Gene Hackman. Now a National Historic Landmark and State Theater of California, the 677-seat venue stages more than 300 performances a year, such as *James and Annie*, by Tony Award-winning playwright Warren Leight, and Claudia Shear's *Dirty Blonde*. The theater also produces new works, many of which have gone on to earn national acclaim.

Must Shop

In a town where actresses are custom-clothed by big-name designers and any savvy salesperson knows who's who in the shop, you can max out your credit card before you know it. From the appointment-only boutiques on Rodeo Drive to the cool shops on Melrose, there's no lack of upscale merchandise in LA. But don't despair if you have a beer budget, there are discounts to be found here, too.

Rodeo Drive★★★

Between Wilshire & Santa Monica Blvds., Beverly Hills. www.rodeodrive.com.

The yardstick by which all other luxury shopping streets in America are measured, Rodeo Drive (say: roe-DAY-oh) holds true to its reputation of "if you have to ask, you can't afford it." From Armani to Zegna, Rodeo ladles up an alphabet soup of famous-name designer boutiques and jewelry stores that stud the three short blocks from Wilshire to Santa Monica boulevards (north of Santa Monica Blvd., Rodeo Drive becomes residential). At least one thing here is not expensive: free parking is available for two hours in the garage on Brighton Way *(off Rodeo Dr.)*.

Via Rodeo – *Northeast corner of Wilshire Blvd. & Rodeo Dr.* More movie set than outdoor mall, tiny Two Rodeo—a.k.a. Via Rodeo—is a boutique-lined cobblestone street, complete with an Italian-village landscape of fountains, piazzas and wrought-iron street lamps.

Rodeo Drive Roster

Here's a sampling of some of the big names you'll find on Rodeo *(in numerical order beginning at the south end of the street)*:

Tiffany *(no. 210)*
Cartier *(nos. 220 & 370)*
José Eber *(no. 224)*
Christian Dior *(no. 230)*
Valentino *(no. 240)*
Van Cleef & Arpels *(no. 300)*
Louis Vuitton *(no. 307)*
David Orgell *(no. 320)*
Georgio *(no. 327)*
Ferragamo *(no. 357)*

Harry Winston *(no. 371)*
Chanel *(no. 400)*
Fred *(no. 401)*
Hermès *(no. 434)*
Armani *(no. 436)*
Gianni Versace *(no. 437)*
Furla *(no. 441)*
Gucci *(no. 443)*
Bottega Veneto *(no. 457)*
Frette *(no. 459)*

World's Most Expensive Store

Looking for something for that special guy? Perhaps a trip to **bijan** is in order. You'll pay up to $15,000 for a suit in this oh-so-exclusive menswear boutique, but isn't he worth it? Don't think you can just drop in, though—shopping at bijan is by appointment only *(420 N. Rodeo Dr.; 310-273-6544; www.bijan.com)*.

Melrose Avenue★

From Doheny Dr. to La Brea Ave, West Hollywood.

On Melrose, shopping is a sport. Choose your weapon: High-end shops crowd the blocks between San Vincente and Robertson, while more affordable off-the-rack and vintage duds fill the small shops farther east. Fashionistas head to Fred Segal *(no. 8100)* and Betsey Johnson *(no. 8050)* to hunt for cutting-edge clothing and to Alan K's *(no. 7380)* to flush out fancy footwear. The herbalist at Elixir

Tea and Tonic *(no. 8512)* can recommend a brew to cure what ails you; take a tea break out back in their peaceful garden.

Soolip Paperie and Press

8648 Melrose Ave. 310-360-0545. www.asoolipwedding.com.

Forget email. Fans of the hand-written word will appreciate the fine assortment of imported papers here. From Italian cotton to Egyptian papyrus, Soolip's selection will astound. If you're in the market for invitations, the store's custom letterpress printing department can do the job for you.

Beverly Center

8500 Beverly Blvd., between La Cienega & San Vicente Blvds. 310-854-0071. www.beverlycenter.com. Open year-round Mon–Fri 10am–9pm, Sat 10am–8pm, Sun 11am–6pm.

Anchored by Macy's and Bloomingdales, some 160 stores and restaurants—including the Hard Rock Cafe and a 13-screen cineplex—sprawl over eight acres in this multi-level indoor mall. A recent renovation has updated the 1982 complex with a new rooftop terrace, which boasts views of the city skyline and the famed Hollywood sign.

The Grove at Farmers Market

Fairfax & Third Sts. 323-900-8080. www.thegrovela.com. Store hours vary.

One of the new favorites for outdoor mall shopping, the Grove is located next to the Original Farmers Market, and close to the museums on Wilshire Boulevard. Here you'll find the likes of Nordstrom, Banana Republic, Abercrombie & Fitch, and Crate & Barrel, along with a new 14-screen movie palace. Trolleys shuttle shoppers between the Grove and the Farmers Market *(see p 87).*

Sunset Plaza

8600-8700 Sunset Blvd., West Hollywood. www.visitwesthollywood.com. Store hours vary.

Residents of nearby Beverly Hills and Bel Air flock to this pedestrian plaza on **Sunset Strip★★** *(see Neighborhoods)* to find the latest fashions from the likes of Dolce & Gabbana, Hervé Leger, Nicole Miller and Anna Sui. When you tire of shopping, the Strip's sidewalk cafes make great spots for star-gazing.

Streets for Shopping

Olvera Street ★

Downtown at El Pueblo de Los Angeles. See Historic Sites.

Shop for authentic Mexican crafts.

Abbot Kinney Boulevard

Between Washington & Venice Blvds., Venice.

Minutes from the boardwalk at Venice Beach, the angled stretch of Abbot Kinney Boulevard has developed into a thriving cosmopolitan street studded with antique- and mod-furnishing finds, one of a kind boutiques (think vintage clothing and lingerie), galleries and cafes. Bring your pooch to the Hydrant Café *(no. 1202)*, where he can lick a cold Frosty Paws while you sip your cappuccino. If you're traveling without your furry friend, try Joe's *(no. 1023)* for innovative California-French cuisine; nibble tapas at Primativo Wine Bistro *(no. 1025)*; or lunch on the patio at Lilly's French Café *(no. 1031)*.

Third Street Promenade ★

Off Arizona Ave. between Wilshire Blvd. & Broadway, Santa Monica. 310-393-8355. www.thirdstreetpromenade.com. Store hours vary.

By day, this open-air pedestrian promenade attracts shoppers to its national retail chains, bookstores and eateries. By night, Third Street Promenade comes alive with a host of street performers, from psychics to singers. Night owls prowl here in the coffee shops, clubs, theaters and cinemas. Anchoring the south end of Third Street Promenade, **Santa Monica Place** was designed by prominent architect Frank Gehry. It offers 140 stores, including department-store chains Macy's and Robinson-May *(on Broadway; 310-319-3080; www.santamonicaplace.com)*.

Bergamot Station Arts Center ★

2525 Michigan Ave., Santa Monica. Open Mon 9am–4pm, Tue–Fri 9am–5pm, Sat 10am–5pm. 310-586-4001. www.bergamotstation.com. Free parking.

A former trolley depot, this group of corrugated steel structures has been transformed into a flower-filled complex of shops and art galleries—33 in all—showcasing work in a variety of media by local and national artists. Sculpture To Wear *(C2)* features lovely art jewelry; the Gallery of Functional Art *(E4)* offers unique home furnishings and accessories. Bergamot Station is also home to the **Santa Monica Museum of Art** *(G1; 310-586-6488; www.smmoa.org)*, which displays changing installations of contemporary art.

Farmers' Markets

Everyone in LA benefits from the agricultural bounty of nearby farmers who bring fresh eggs, jams, cheeses, honeys, and heaps of just-picked produce to the nearly 100 open-air markets held in neighborhoods around the city each week. Here are a few of our favorites:

Grand Central Market★ – *317 S. Broadway at Hill St., opposite California Plaza. 213-624-2378. www.grandcentralsquare.com. Open year-round daily 9am–6pm. See Landmarks.* Located in downtown LA, Grand Central dates back to 1917. Aside from the usual produce, flowers, meats and cheeses, you can get great ethnic cuisine here—cheap. Buy a burrito, a bowl of wonton soup or a Cuban sandwich and enjoy your meal at communal tables in the Market Court, where you'll have a view of the Angel's Flight railway *(see Landmarks)*.

Original Farmers Market★ – *6333 W. 3rd St. at Fairfax St., West Hollywood. 323-933-9211. www.farmersmarketla.com. Open year-round Mon–Fri 9am– 9pm, Sat 9am–8pm, Sun 10am–7pm.* Since it opened in 1934, the original Farmers Market has been the source for fresh fruits and vegetables, seafood and meats in LA. While you shop for artisanal cheese at Monsieur Marcel Gourmet Market *(www.mrmarcel.com),* you can station the kids outside the windows at Bennett's to watch ice cream being made by hand.

Beverly Hills Farmers' Market – *200 block of N. Canon Dr. 310-550-4796. Open Sun 9am–1pm.* Every Sunday, rain or shine, the Beverly Hills market hosts some 60 farmers and vendors. Come mingle with the locals and feast on freshly made tamales, crepes or soups.

Santa Monica Farmers' Market – *2nd St. & Arizona Ave. 310-458-8712. http://farmersmarket.santa-monica.org. Open Wed 9am–2pm & Sat 8:30am–1pm. Check online for other locations.* Markets in Santa Monica are known city-wide for their grand scale and their abundance of farm-fresh fruits, vegetables and eggs. More than 60 percent of the produce sold at the Saturday market is organically grown.

Perhaps nowhere do the words "must be seen" ring as true as they do in LA, where the real stars come out after midnight. The hippest bars and clubs are concentrated in West Hollywood and Hollywood, so if you want to get in, the dress is tight and trendy. Admission fees and drink minimums vary, depending upon who's doing the entertaining that night. Call to ask about age requirements (in some places you must be 21 to get in).

The Avalon

1735 Vine St. at Hollywood Blvd. 323-462-8900. www.avalonhollywood.com.

Born as the Hollywood Palace theater in 1927, the Avalon now entertains with DJs and live bands at Hollywood and Vine. The Beatles played their first West Coast gig here in 1964; more recent performers have included the Beastie Boys, The Dan Band and Nickel Creek. On Friday nights, the resident DJ spins dance music from hip-hop to rock.

Beauty Bar

1638 Cahuenga Blvd., Hollywood. 323-464-7676. www.beautybar.com. Open Sun–Wed 8pm–2am. Manicures available Thu–Sat 6pm–2am.

Go with a gal pal. Sit under a hair dryer, sip a martini, and enjoy the mid-1960s beauty-salon vibe. Come on, get in the spirit with a Platinum Blonde (Stoli vodka, Malibu rum and pineapple juice). During Manicure and Martini Happy Hour *(Thu & Fri after 6pm & Sat 8pm–11pm)*, if you buy a $10 cocktail, you get a free manicure.

B.B. King's Blues Club & Restaurant

100 Universal City Plaza, at Universal Studios CityWalk. 818-622-5464. www.universalstudios.com.

You never know who'll be sitting with the band at this Memphis-influenced blues club at Universal Studios Hollywood. B.B. King's presents live music seven nights a week along with an authentic Creole menu. It's quiet for dinner early in the evening and livens up after 9pm, when the local dating crowd replaces the theme-park tourists.

Forty Deuce

5574 Melrose Ave., Hollywood. 323-465-4242. www.fortydeuce.com.

This speakeasy-style hotspot on Melrose is a burlesque boite where dancer Carolina works her way across the horseshoe-shaped bar to the rhythm of a jazz trio. Justin Timberlake liked her enough to ask her to appear in his video. You're sure to recognize some of the regulars here.

House of Blues

8430 Sunset Blvd., West Hollywood. 323-848-5100. www.hob.com.

Top performers, from Natalie Cole and Eric Clapton to Liz Phair and Dave Matthews—have all played at House of Blues, where the live-music schedule boasts big names as well as local talent. The Sunday Gospel Brunch *(10am & 1pm)* may set your toes a-tapping, but this place really gets to rocking late at night.

Key Club

9039 Sunset Blvd., West Hollywood. 310-274-5800. www.keyclub.com.

This popular Sunset Strip venue wins raves from local press for being the best place to hear live music in LA. With its state-of-the-art sound system, good sight lines, and capacity for 500 people, the Key Club consistently packs them in. Recent performers have included LA Guns, the Gin Blossoms and Marcia Ball. The club's acclaimed restaurant serves American fare until midnight. Downstairs, there's a room where you can just hang out with friends.

Linq Restaurant and Lounge

8338 W. 3rd St., West Hollywood. 323-655-4555. www.linqlounge.com.

Restaurateur Mario Oliver created the concept, and designer *du jour* Dodd Mitchell outfitted the chic minimalist space with brown-velvet couches and white lacquered tables. A glass-domed atrium in the restaurant allows diners to eat under the twinkling stars. On Thursday and Friday nights, the lounge, with its 35ft-long bottom-lit teak bar, becomes a lively late-night spot where DJs spin tunes.

Lunaria

10351 Santa Monica Blvd., Century City. 310-282-8870. www.lunariajazzscene.com.

After feasting on Provencal cuisine, the dining-room doors swing open and it's time for jazz (bluegrass on Tuesday). Frank Sinatra Jr. has performed here and George Segal once played his banjo with the onstage bluegrass group. Recent acts have included Conrad Janis and acclaimed blues artist, Peach.

Nacional

1645 Wilcox Ave., Hollywood. 323-962-7712.

The theme may be 1950s Havana, but be forewarned that the door policy is not exactly open to all (it helps to know someone). If you do get in, a DJ creates the sounds while you sip a mojito, dance the salsa or just groove to the beat. It's *the* place to dance on Tuesday night.

Pearl

665 N Robertson Blvd., West Hollywood. 310-358-9191. www.pearl90069.com.

When live bands aren't playing here, erotic dancers writhe behind shadow-boxes on the performance stage. Two DJ stations, six plasma screens and 100 speakers insure that the joint will be jumping. If that's not enough, there's "Sinferno" nights, with sexy vaudeville acts, and "Karaoke from Hell," your opportunity to sing with a live band.

The Roxy Theatre

9009 Sunset Blvd., Hollywood. 310-279-9457. www.theroxyonsunset.com.

This small club is a remnant of the 1960s, when its stage played host to John Lennon and James Taylor. Today it's mostly local bands that play the Roxy. With a seating capacity of 250, it's an intimate venue in which to catch up-and-coming musicians.

The Standard

8300 Sunset Blvd., West Hollywood. 323-650-9090. www.standardhotel.com.

It's a hip and happening bar scene at this Sunset Strip hotel. Plus, there's a cool diner-like coffee shop that serves 24/7. The international menu includes classic American fare such as burger and fries.

Viper Room

8852 Sunset Blvd., West Hollywood. 310-358-1880. www.viperroom.com.

Actor Johnny Depp co-owns this West Hollywood favorite on Sunset Strip. Eddie Vedder, Johnny Cash, Mick Jagger and Dwight Yoakam have all put in appearances here, many unannounced. The action takes place upstairs, but you can watch the performances on video monitors in the downstairs bar if you can't get tickets to the show.

Swingers Diner

8020 Beverly Blvd., in the Beverly Laurel Motor Hotel, West Hollywood. 323-653-5858. www.swingersdiner.com.

Did all that partying make you hungry? For those late-night munchies, try Swingers. Diner fare here includes everything from burgers and chili dogs to a tofu breakfast sauté. Wash down your choice with a thick milkshake or a smoothie. Last call for wine and beer is 1:30am, but you can order food until 4am.

Whisky A Go-Go

8901 Sunset Blvd. at San Vicente Blvd., Hollywood. 310-652-4202.
www.whiskyagogo.com.

The birthplace of go-go dancing in the 1960s is now a Sunset Strip icon for rock aficionados who love live bands—as many as six play here on any given weekend night. Jim Morrison and the Doors was once the house band here; now, new and emerging artists entertain along with famous ones.

Whiskey Bar

1200 Alta Loma Rd., in the Sunset Marquis Hotel, West Hollywood. 310-657-1333.
www.sunsetmarquishotel.com.

This sophisticated velvet-rope club in the Sunset Marquis Hotel draws an A-list of celebrities who mingle after midnight with music legends. The sexy, dimly lit room, with its wall-length banquettes, provides a comfy place to mellow out. If your favorite singer shows up, just be cool and pretend not to notice.

White Lotus

1743 N. Cahuenga Blvd., Hollywood. 323-463-0060.
www.whitelotushollywood.com.

Late-night Hollywood sizzles in this bar with its long sake list and a sushi, dim sum and then-some menu. Across the foyer, the dance club features two bars, and DJs who spin Top 40, hip-hop, trance and house music. And it's all designed to have good feng shui, although the crowd on the dance floor doesn't seem to care.

Comedy Clubs

Comedy and Magic Club

1018 Hermosa Ave., Hermosa Beach. 310-372-1193. www.comedyandmagicclub.com.

When Jay Leno isn't taping *The Tonight Show*, he can often be found trying out his material here on Sundays nights. Since 1978, this 225-seat South Bay club has hosted the likes of comedic greats Robin Williams, Jim Carrey, Jerry Seinfeld and Billy Crystal.

Hollywood Improv

8162 Melrose Ave., Hollywood. 323-651-2583. www.hollywoodimprov.com.

Budd Friedman has been providing a venue for up-and-coming comedians since he started the Improv in Manhattan in 1963. You'll recognize the brick wall in Hollywood as the backdrop for the *Live at the Improv* tapings. Rosie O'Donnell, Robin Williams, Adam Sandler and Drew Carey have all graced the Improv stage. On any given night, you'll laugh out loud with 10 comic performers.

s it *really* better to look good than to feel good? You be the judge. LA's myriad pampering palaces cater to the glitterati as well as to weary travelers. When driving around the freeways stresses you out, soothe your body and soul at one of these prestigious spas . . . Oh, and, darling, you look maahvelous!

Amadeus Spa

799 E. Green St., Pasadena. 626-578-3404. www.amadeusspa.com.

Treatments take on an international air at Amadeus. Experience the Middle East with a Dead Sea rejuvenation (using salt and mud from the Dead Sea), rebalance your energy with Asian yin/yang or detox with seaweed from France's Brittany coast. And what would a trip to the home of the Rose Bowl be without the Pasadena Rose, a soak in rose-scented waters followed by a rose-oil massage?

Beverly Hills Hotel Spa by La Prairie

9641 Sunset Blvd., Beverly Hills. 310-276-2251. www.beverlyhillshotel.com.

Opened in February 2004, this spa features luxuriant treatments using the famed La Prairie line of skin-care products. Just got into town? Go for the jet-lag therapy, 90 minutes of bliss, with an aromatherapy massage, hand and foot reflexology, and a facial. The cognoscenti come here for pre-party glamorizing, as well as for treatments like caviar firming facials and Diamond Perfection—a micro-dermabrasion for the entire body.

Fred Segal Beauty Salon & Spa

420 Broadway, Santa Monica. 310-451-5155. www.fredsegalbeauty.com.

Splurge on a day of beauty at Fred Segal. From hair design and nails to no-nonsense facials and body treatments, you can have it all done here. Customize your own massage with a combination of techniques including Thai yoga massage, reflexology, Shiatsu, Lomi Lomi, and even pregnancy massage. Got a special occasion coming up? Let the salon's consultants create a whole new image for you.

The Humble Abode Day Spa and Salon

519 N. La Cienega, Suite 9, West Hollywood. 310-360-9300. www.thehumbleabode.com.

The staff at the Humble Abode devotes itself to preventative care and well-being with a menu of services from chiropractic care to gimmick-free deep-cleansing facials and a hair and nail salon. Go for a spa package like the Core Beauty Retreat—including a private Pilates session, a facial and an hour-long massage—or create your own day of pampering by picking three or more of your favorite treatments.

Kinara Spa

656 N. Robertson Blvd., West Hollywood. 310-657-9188. www.kinaraspa.com.

This Design District retreat was created by Christine Splichal (wife of famed chef Joachim Splichal) and her former aesthetician, Olga Lorencin-Northrup. Together they operate a popular day spa, gift shop and cafe in a spacious storefront between Melrose Avenue and Santa Monica Boulevard. Locals and celebs—Halle Berry, Anjelica Houston and Christina Applegate—favor Lorencin-Northrup's traditional Eastern European skin-care services and products in the spa, and savor Splichal's mostly organic Zone-friendly fare in the outdoor garden.

The Peninsula Spa

9882 Little Santa Monica Blvd., at the Peninsula Beverly Hills, Beverly Hills. 310-551-2888 or 800-462-7899. www.peninsula.com.

Shhh . . . Regulars like to keep the rooftop spa at the Peninsula hotel as their little secret. This intimate spa is open to the public, of course, with two-week advance appointments. If you can't make it to the South Pacific this year, try the Delice de Tahiti; you'll be scrubbed with warm kukui oil, toned with noni gel, and wrapped in banana leaves. Moonlight massages in the poolside cabanas set the stage for romance.

Spa at Le Merigot

1740 Ocean Ave., Santa Monica. 310-395-9700 or 800-228-9292. www.lemerigothotel.com.

Start your session here with a workout at the poolside cardio deck, just a short stroll from the beach. The 5,500sq ft European-style spa features salt glows and body polishes, herbal baths and body bronzing, and even a fitness facial for men. Massage choices range from hot-stone to Reiki and Cranial Sacral therapy. For the cost of a treatment, you'll get access to the hotel's health club, sauna, steam room and pool—not to mention a comfy robe and slippers.

Spa at the Four Seasons Hotel Los Angeles at Beverly Hills

300 South Doheny Dr., Beverly Hills. 310-273-2222. www.fourseasons.com.

Take a eucalyptus steam; sip ginger tea; revel in a deep-tissue massage in the poolside cabana. These are sure to become a few of your favorite things at the Four Seasons' fourth-floor spa. The house specialty, the Punta Mita massage, is good for what ails you. The healing properties of tequila and sage oil combine in this detoxifying treatment, which is designed to improve circulation and digestion. Other indulgent services include facials, manicures, pedicures and foot reflexology, plus a full menu of massages—some with custom-blended aromatherapy oils.

The Spa at the Regent Beverly Wilshire

9500 Wilshire Blvd., Beverly Hills. 310-275-5200 or 800-427-4354. www.regenthotels.com.

Located on the second floor of the hotel's Beverly Wing, the spa welcomes day guests and offers everything from an hour to a Day of Beauty to a Pretty Woman Suite Getaway. They offer a full array of spa treatments, including a choice of massages, body wraps and facials—plus salon services at the new Sylvain Melloul Salon. Spa guests can use the pool and the fitness facility.

Spa Mystique

10220 Constellation Ave., in the Century Plaza Hotel, Century City. 310-551-3251. www.spamystique.com.

Occupying a 35,000sq ft space in the Century Plaza Hotel, Spa Mystique gives clients their choice of treatment venues between 27 indoor rooms and 4 outdoor cabanas. Services here echo Eastern rituals; try the Royal Journey package, a half-day of luxury beginning with a Sleeping Tiger massage, followed by a lotus flower body wrap and a yin/yang facial. Before your

Yamaguchi Salon

Renowned stylist Billy Yamaguchi's salon concept incorporates a holistic approach to looking good. Whether you go for a cut and color, a centering manicure, a tea pedicure, or a feng shui beauty consultation, you're bound to leave looking—and feeling—good.

treatment, pump some iron in the fitness center or check out the fabulous selection of classes—from body sculpting to yoga.

St. Regis Spa

2055 Avenue of the Stars, in the St. Regis Hotel, Century City. 310-277-6111. www.stregis.com.

The private 2,000sq ft spa was created in 2000, when the Century Towers building was transformed into the St. Regis hotel. Work out in the state-of-the-art fitness center with its curved, glass wall looking out to the new pool, cabanas and whirlpool. Then sample the sauna and steam rooms, before treating yourself to a facial, massage, or a body exfoliation. The spa tailors its services to both men and women.

Spa Getaways

Sometimes, you need to indulge your spirit for more than a day. When you really want to escape, head two hours south of LA to the north end of San Diego County, for a splurge at one of these over-the-top spa destinations.

Cal-a-Vie

29402 Spa Havens Way, Vista, CA. 760-945-2055 or 866-772-4283. www.cal-a-vie.com.

You'll feel like you're in Provence when you see this rose-covered hillside hideaway. Most of the 24 guests here try to improve their personal lifestyle goals—lose weight, jump-start a fitness campaign or reduce stress. Some simply come to escape. Chef Steve Pernetti's food and Friday cooking class are fabulous, and each of the villas, newly renovated with French antiques, has a private terrace or balcony. You'll start your day here with a wake-up walk and then move on to fitness classes. After lunch on the outdoor patio, it's time to hit the spa—at last!

Golden Door

777 Deer Springs Rd. San Marcos, CA. 760-744-5777 or 800-424-0777. www.goldendoor.com.

You won't be bored at this all-inclusive seven-day beauty boot camp, where your day starts with a hike at dawn. Designed for women, the spa caters to 40 guests at a time with a 4-to-1 staff-to-guest ratio. Try T'ai Chi, do yoga, meditate, dance, or take a private tennis lesson . . . the possibilities are nearly limitless. You'll be paired with a personal fitness counselor who will outline a regimen of increasing intensity; nutritionists will plan your meals, according to the goals you set for yourself. All the while, you'll be cosseted on a 377-acre retreat amid groves of citrus and avocado trees, gentle waterfalls and traditional Japanese gardens. Ah, serenity.

Spa La Costa

At the La Costa Resort and Spa, Costa Del Mar Rd., Carlsbad, CA. 760-438-9111 or 800-854-5000. www.lacosta.com.

Even spa resorts need a facelift once in a while. One of the country's first (1965) and favorite golf-resort spas, La Costa got a $140 million makeover in March 2004. Housed in Spanish Colonial-style white-stucco buildings, the new 28,000sq ft spa, incorporates 42 treatment rooms and a large outdoor courtyard with a pool and waterfall. Services here all begin with the complementary Agua de la Vida bathing ritual: a soak in the whirlpool, a session under the massaging waters of the Roman waterfall, an exfoliating body scrub, and time to relax in the cedar sauna and steam room. You can add to your spa stay by taking advantage of the holistic health programs at the Chopra Center (named for New Age wellness guru Deepak Chopra), also housed at the resort.

Want to cruise to an offshore island or rock-climb in the desert? Want to frolic with cartoon characters or golf in a valley surrounded by snow-capped peaks? Within two hours of LA, you can visit one of the world's most popular theme parks, go back in time to historic missions or escape to an exclusive resort.

Disneyland Resort★★★

Anaheim, site of the Disney theme parks (Disneyland Resort & Disney's California Adventure), is located 25mi southeast of LA. Take I-5 south to the Disneyland exit. 714-781-7290 (operator-assisted) or 714-781-4565 (recorded information). www.disneyland.com.

Mickey, Minnie, Donald Duck, Pluto—who could have imagined that a few friendly cartoon characters could give rise to a global empire? Walter Elias Disney, that's who. Born and raised in the Midwest, the cartoonist (1901–1966) took his first animation job in Kansas City at the age of 18 and founded his own production company in 1922. By 1923 Walt and his brother Roy, now in Hollywood, had established the Disney Brothers Studio. They scored their first box-office success in 1928 with *Steamboat Willie,* a cartoon starring the newly created character Mickey Mouse. Other smash hits followed.

In the early 1950s, Walt purchased a tract of orange groves in Anaheim and formed a team of "Imagineers" to design his wildly popular Magic Kingdom. In 2001, after a $1.4-billion expansion, the original 90-acre park was joined by a second theme park, 55-acre Disney's California Adventure. Linking the two is **Downtown Disney,** a shopping, dining, and entertainment district best enjoyed in the evening. The three parts now make up the massive Disneyland Resort.

Tips for Visiting

When to go – To avoid the biggest crowds, visit between September and March, excluding holidays. If you must visit during the summer or on a holiday, go on a weekday. Arrive either an hour before the parks open or an hour afterward.

Ticket options – One-day tickets *($49.75 adults; $39.75 children ages 3–9)* will get you into either Disneyland Park or Disney's California Adventure, not both. Two-day Park Hopper passes *($98 adults; $78 children ages 3–9)* allow you to go back and forth between parks.

FastPass – Slip your ticket into a FastPass terminal at, say, Space Mountain, and it will spit out a reservation time so you can enjoy the park rather than stand in line.

Disneyland Park★★★

1313 Harbor Blvd, Anaheim. Open daily year-round. Hours vary considerably; call or consult Web site for schedule.

Roughly elliptical in shape, Disneyland is organized into eight distinct sections that radiate out from the Central Plaza.

Adventureland – The Indiana Jones Adventure (think spiders, snakes and skulls) and the Jungle Cruise (surfin' safari) are the favorites here.

Critter Country – Expect to get wet as you swish down Splash Mountain in a log boat at a top speed of 40mph.

Fantasyland – While some find it cloying, It's a Small World, an audio-animatronic® boat tour, remains a perennial favorite. Watch a musical version of Snow White, or experience the Matterhorn Mountain roller coaster.

Frontierland – Big Thunder Mountain Railroad is a thrill ride (tame by today's standards) on a simulated runaway train. At night, visitors crowd the shoreline to see *Fantasmic*, a fiber-optic show.

Main Street, U.S.A. – Horse-drawn trolleys, fire engines and a double-decker bus ferry passengers past tidy brick Victorians holding old-fashioned shops, mom-and-pop soda fountains, a penny arcade and a cinema.

Mickey's Toontown – Roger Rabbit's Car Toon Spin offers a harrowing adventure through this 1930s cartoon come-to-life.

New Orleans Square – Strolling musicians perform Dixieland jazz in this squeaky-clean version of New Orleans' French Quarter. Go a-raidin' with a rollicking crew of rum-runners in the wildly popular Pirates of the Caribbean.

Tomorrowland – This "classic future environment" features the roller-coaster Space Mountain *(closed until 2005)*; Star Tours, a *Star Wars*-themed virtual voyage; and *Honey, I Shrunk the Audience,* a 3-D film.

Disney's California Adventure★★

Adjacent to Disneyland. 714-781-7290 (operator-assisted) or 714-781-4565 (recorded information). www.disneyland.com. Hours vary.

Disney's Grand Californian Hotel

1600 Disneyland Dr., Anaheim. 714-956-6425. www.disneyland.com

The design of Disneyland's newest hotel, a deluxe resort with six stories and 751 rooms, was inspired by the California Arts & Crafts movement. A bungalow-style porte-cochere greets guests arriving at the front entrance. The lobby's timbered ceiling soars 753ft. Within the hotel, the award-winning **Napa Rose** restaurant features fresh, local products, from white asparagus to Chardonnay. Guestrooms go for about $235–$330; call and ask about package deals. The Grand Californian is the only hotel with a private entrance to both parks.

Disney's newest theme park explores the richness and diversity of California. It goes lighter on the fairy tales than its 50-year-old neighbor and heavier on the reality of the State: high-tech innovation (translated here as awesome special effects and stomach-dropping rides) and high-toned tastes (sourdough bread and Napa Valley wine). The park is divided into four "lands."

A Bug's Land – Insect exploration for the very young.

The Golden State – Try hiking and white-water rafting on Grizzly River Run; Napa Valley tastings at the Golden Vine Winery; and seafood with sourdough on Pacific Wharf, reminiscent of Monterey's Cannery Row. Soarin' over California is a dizzying hang-gliding tour of the state, complete with the scent of orange blossoms.

Hollywood Pictures Backlot – A tribute to the golden era of filmmaking—the two-block version of Hollywood Boulevard includes Disney's animation studio and live-entertainment theater. Opened in 2004, Twilight Zone Tower of Terror is the park's newest and scariest ride.

Paradise Pier – Thrill seekers flock to this beachfront amusement zone. California Screamin' is a roller coaster that accelerates from zero to 55mph in less than five seconds.

Not in a mousy mood?

Consider these other Anaheim-area sites:

Crystal Cathedral★ – *12141 Lewis St., Garden Grove. 714-971-4000. www.crystalcathedral.org. Open year-round daily Mon–Sat 9am–3:30pm, Sun 6am–9pm.* Architect Richard Neutra designed this star-shaped, glass-walled cathedral in 1961, and Phillip Johnson conceived the 3,000-seat "sanctuary" in 1980. You needn't go inside for services: 1,400 parking spaces allow visitors to view the pulpit on a huge outdoor video screen and participate in the service from their cars.

Richard Nixon Library & Birthplace★ – *18001 Yorba Linda Blvd., Yorba Linda. 714-993-3393. www.nixonfoundation.org. $5.95.* Letters, papers, vintage film clips, and audiotape (including the Watergate "smoking gun") explore the life of the enigmatic president, who was born here in 1913.

Joshua Tree National Park★★

140mi east of Los Angeles via I-10 & Rte 62. 760-367-7511 www.nps.gov/jotr. The park's three visitor centers are open daily year-round 8am–4pm (Oasis Visitor Center open until 5pm). $10 per vehicle (for 7 days). Campsites are the only accommodations in the park; bring your own food and plenty of water.

The huge national park is a natural arid haven from the commercial concentration that winds its way up and down the coast. Rock climbers, campers and day trippers are as attracted to the park's remoteness—it covers 558,000 acres—as they are to the distinctive twisted form of the tree that devout Mormons named Joshua after the Biblical prophet.

Keys View★★ – At 5,185ft, this perch on the crest of the Little San Bernardino Mountains offers a sweeping view of Coachella Valley.

Cholla Cactus Garden★ – Cholla grows here in great abundance, thanks to favorable ground-water conditions.

Geology Tour Road★ – The rugged and scenic 18mi dirt road is marked with 16 stops that highlight evidence of the geological forces present. A four-wheel drive vehicle is recommended.

Hidden Valley Nature Trail★ – An easy 1mi loop trail winds through a natural enclosure formed by hills of monzogranite where cattle rustlers allegedly hid stolen cattle in the 1880s. Today the area is a mecca for rock climbers.

Walks Among the Rocks★ – These short nature trails, several with interpretive signs identifying desert plants, provide easy access to mysteriously attractive quartz monzogranite formations.

Palm Springs★★

110mi southwest of Los Angeles via I-10. Tourist information: 777 N. Palm Canyon Dr. or 2701 Palm Canyon Dr.; 800-927-7256; www.palm-springs.org.

Fans of sunshine enjoy rays about 354 days a year here. Popularly known as the golf capital of the world (there are 110 courses), this city of 44,000 people forms an upscale oasis of lush greenery, splendid spas and snow-capped peaks amid arid desert. The high season runs from January to May; there's plenty to do in the summer months too, but the heat can be beastly.

The **Uptown Palm Springs Heritage District** is rife with modernist architectural gems; shops specialize in mid-20C furnishings. On Palm Canyon Drive, the city's Main Street, you'll find a **visitor center** *(no. 777)* and the **Walk of Stars**, which honors entertainment personalities in bronze. Thanks to the profusion of propertied Indian tribes (and opportunistic developers) in the region, Palm Springs also sports four **casinos**. In neighboring Palm Desert you'll find **El Paseo,** a 2mi-long boulevard lined with chic boutiques.

Palm Springs Aerial Tramway★★★

One Tramway Rd. 760-325-1449. www.pstramway.com. Open year-round Mon–Fri 10am–9:45pm; weekends 8am-9:45pm. $20.80.

This is one of the most amazing 10-minute rides you're likely to experience anywhere. Revolving, 80-passenger gondolas (the largest in the world) ascend the vertiginous face of San Jacinto, letting you watch as the desert heat gives way to the mountain cold. En route, spectacular **views**★★ extend for miles around. Up top you can eat at the Top of The Tram restaurant and hike or cross-country ski, depending on the season, on 54mi of trails covering 13,000 acres.

Palm Springs Desert Museum★★

101 Museum Dr. 760-325-7186. www.psmuseum.org. Open year-round Tue, Wed, Fri & Sat 10am–5pm, Thu noon–8pm, Sun noon–5pm. Closed major holidays. $7.50.

Housed in a polished contemporary structure, this museum, founded in 1938, offers an excellent overview of the natural history, cultural history and art of the California deserts.

- **Natural science wing –** Dioramas, displays and terrariums describe desert ecology.

- **Art collections –** The focus is on 20C California art and sculpture, with works by Henry Moore and Dale Chihuly.

> **Viceroy Palm Springs**
>
> *415 S. Belardo Rd. 800-237-3687. www.viceroypalmsprings.com.*
>
> Designed in a modern interpretation of the Hollywood Regency style with a color palette of white, lemon yellow and black, the Viceroy Palm Springs is a refuge replete with private villas, manicured grounds, three refreshing pools and a delicious spa. Stay to enjoy a martini and dine at Citron, a happening restaurant offering Cal-French classics.

Living Desert Zoo and Gardens★★

15mi east of Palm Springs in Palm Desert. 760-346-5694. www.livingdesert.org. Open Sept–mid-Jun daily 9am–5pm. Rest of the year 8am–1:30pm. Closed Dec 25. $10.50.

Great for kids, this 1,200-acre nature preserve, an important conservation center, gives you an up-close look at desert flora and fauna.

- **Animals –** 425 animals represent 145 species, including Mexican wolves, bighorn sheep, coyotes, oryx, zebras, cheetahs, mountain lions and a golden eagle.

- **Gardens –** 1,500 varieties of plants are arranged in 10 different ecosystems.

Santa Barbara★★

About 90mi northwest of Los Angeles via US-101 (the Ventura Freeway) north. Tourist information: 805-966-9222 or 800-676-1266; www.santabarbaraca.com.

Red-tile roofs, white-washed stucco buildings and palm-fringed beaches give this chic yet relaxed enclave a distinctively Mediterranean feel. The Spanish staked their claim here in the late 18C, building a presidio and a mission. A century later, wealthy Americans, many from the East, got wind of the area's mild climate and the health-promoting mineral springs, and began coming here in droves via a new branch of the Southern Pacific Railroad.

After a severe earthquake leveled the business district in 1925, residents rebuilt in the Spanish Colonial Revival style, a look that today extends from the biggest adobe structure to the smallest mailbox. The downtown lends itself to walking: State Street is the main thoroughfare, connecting an upscale shopping district *(bounded by Ortega and Victoria Sts.)* to historic Stearns Wharf *(see p 102)*.

Mission Santa Bárbara★★★

2201 Laguna St. 805-682-4713. www.sbmission.org. Open year-round daily 9am–5pm. Services Sat & Sun. Call for times.

Rising up majestically against the Santa Ynez foothills, the twin bell towers of "the queen of the missions" attest to the city's remarkable continuity. Throughout its 225-year history, the mission has never ceased to serve as a parish church, and today it remains a vibrant part of the community. The first church, erected in 1787, was replaced three times by larger structures, all of which anchored a complex of about 250 adobe dwellings for the Chumash Indians ("neophytes" in the missionaries' parlance). Then, in 1812, a severe earthquake destroyed the site, which had to be rebuilt from the ground up.

The church you see today dates from 1820. Inside, the painted canvas reredos (1806) formed the basis for the detailed design scheme. In the **Padres' Quarters** you'll find a collection of mission artifacts from the late 18C to the early 19C. Note especially the 1792 psalter (book of psalms), with its 75 hand-lettered sheepskin pages.

Santa Barbara County Courthouse★★

1100 Anacapa St. 805-962-6464. www.sbcourts.org. Open year-round Mon–Fri 8:30am–4:30pm, weekends 10am–4:30pm. Free tours Mon–Fri at 10:30am & 2pm, Sun 2pm. Closed Dec 25.

Shining star of Santa Barbara's architectural renaissance, the L-shaped Moorish structure (1929) boasts arched doorways, open-air galleries and Tunisian tile and metalwork; even elements such as telephone booths are cached in carved wood frames. The building surrounds a sunken courtyard.

Observation deck – Go to the top of the 85ft clock tower for **panoramic views★★** of the city.

Santa Barbara Museum of Art★

1130 State St. 805-963-4364. www.sbmuseart.org. Open year-round Tue–Sat 11am 5pm (Fri until 9pm); Sun noon–5pm. $7.

Housed in an elegant Italian Renaissance-style building, this is one of the country's best regional art museums. Thirteen galleries showcase 4,500 years of Asian, European and American art, with a curatorial eye toward educating and inspiring visitors.

Main level – Works range from Greek and Roman antiquities to the present. Note especially the rotating thematic and one-artist exhibitions of California art, a specialty of the museum.

Upper level – The Asian art collection embraces cultural artifacts from Japan to India. Photography is displayed in the Sterling Morton Gallery.

Santa Barbara Museum of Natural History★

2559 Puesta del Sol. 805-682-4711. www.sbnature.org. Open year-round daily 10am–5pm. Closed Jan 1, Thanksgiving Day & Dec 25. $6.

Exhibits at the museum, founded in 1914, focus on the flora, fauna, geology and ethnography of the West Coast. The site itself is worth a look: the complex of Spanish-style stucco buildings is set on 11 beautiful acres of wooded canyon. Highlights include the **Chumash Indian Hall,** which contains the state's largest collection of artifacts from this tribe; the massive skeleton of a **blue whale;** a **planetarium** *(call for show times);* and a superb roster of special exhibitions.

Stearns Wharf★

At the foot of State Street juts this 2,604ft landmark (1872), the oldest working wharf in California. Now lined with shops and restaurants, it's a fun place to shop and snack and watch fishermen unload their daily catch. There are also exhibits on local wildlife.

Catalina Island★

Santa Catalina Island lies 21mi off the California coast south of Los Angeles. Passenger ferries link Avalon with Long Beach, Dana Point, San Pedro and Newport Beach (see sidebar, below). Automobiles are not allowed. Catalina Island Visitors Bureau and Chamber of Commerce is located at 1 Green Pleasure Pier, Avalon; 310-510-1520; www.catalina.com.

With its 54mi of rugged coastline, this magical, mountainous isle (pop. 3,000) is a great place to get away from the city streets. Hugging the hillsides surrounding the bay, Avalon—Catalina's only town—is a tightly packed assortment of pastel-colored bungalows, hotels, restaurants and souvenir shops. Inland you'll find some excellent natural areas. The **Wrigley Memorial and Botanical Garden** *(1400 Avalon Canyon Rd.; 310-510-2288)* highlights the island's native plants. A quarter-mile below the garden is the **Santa Catalina Island Interpretive Center** *(310-510-2514)*, which examines the island's ecology and provides hiking permits *(free)*, maps and trail information. Check out the excellent **boat trips** and **harbor cruises.**

Casino Building★★

1 Casino Way, Avalon. Visit by 50-minute guided tour only; call for times; reservations required. 310-510-7400. www.catalina.com. $12.75 (includes museum admission).

The 140ft-tall circular Art Deco landmark (1929) had its heyday in the 1930s and 40s, when big band legends such as Benny Goodman played here to legions of music lovers from the mainland.

Ferries

Ferry service to the island costs about $42 per adult round-trip; travel time is 1hr to 1hr 45min each way. Parking at ferry terminals is about $8 a day. Check in at least 45 minutes before departure. Catalina Express *(310-519-1212 or 800-481-3470; www.catalinaexpress.com)* offers up to 30 daily departures from San Pedro and Long Beach *(see Beach Communities)*. Catalina Flyer *(949-673-5245; www.catalinainfo.com)* departs from Balboa Pavilion in Newport Beach *(see p 105)*.

Laguna Beach★

90mi south of LA via I-405 to Hwy. 133/Laguna Beach exit. Proceed south to the Pacific Coast Hwy. Laguna Beach Visitor's Bureau is located at 252 Broadway; 800-877-1115; www.lagunabeachinfo.org.

A picture-postcard-perfect coastal community, Laguna Beach is an idyllic seaside haven that's long been popular with painters and Hollywood types. Rocky canyons studded with lagoons gave the town its name. Steep hillsides rise to about 1,000ft above the ocean, so the quaint, tree-shaded homes have magnificent ocean views. You can walk the boardwalk, hit the beach, kayak in the ocean, bike the hillsides, shop in the boutiques and 40 art galleries or lounge at a seaside restaurant. In summer, crowds flock here for major art events, such as the **Festival of Arts and Pageant of the Masters** *(800-487-3378; pageanttickets.com),* where visitors can buy paintings or watch performers re-create them in nightly *tableaux vivants* (living pictures).

Laguna Art Museum★

307 Cliff Dr. 949-494-8971. www.lagunaartmuseum.org. Open year-round Thu–Tue 11am–5pm. $7.

Founded in 1918 as the Laguna Art Association, the museum was formed to champion local artists and their work. While both its facilities and its scope have expanded—all American artists are welcomed now, though Californians are preferred—it remains a fixture in the community. Rotating exhibits run the gamut from the historical to the cutting edge.

Mission San Juan Capistrano★★

8mi south of Laguna Beach in San Juan Capistrano. 949-234-1300. www.missionsjc.com. Open year-round daily 8:30am–5pm. Closed Good Friday afternoon, Thanksgiving Day & Dec 25. $6. The ruins of the **Great Stone Church** lend a mysterious and historic air to this quiet town of 31,000. The mission was founded by Padre Junipero Serra in 1775 with the intent of converting the natives, or "neophytes," to Christianity and establishing a Spanish presence in the area. The church was completed, after 10 years of construction, in 1806, only to be toppled by an earthquake in 1812.

Newport Beach★

45mi south of Los Angeles via I-405 to Fwy. 55 South (which becomes Newport Blvd.). Newport Blvd. leads to Balboa Blvd., which runs the length of Balboa Peninsula. Tourist information: Newport Beach Conference & Visitors Bureau; 949-719-6100 or 800-942-6278; www.newportbeach-cvb.com.

When you enter Newport Beach from the highway, it looks like any sprawling suburban community in California. Never fear. Just head to Balboa Peninsula, the city's sun-bleached soul. This thin spit of land runs east-west along the mainland, cupping what is now the largest small-boat harbor in the world. Along the peninsula's southern (ocean) side is a 6mi sandy beach bracketed by historic piers on either end. Extending along the bayfront next to the 1904 **Balboa Pavilion**★ *(400 Main St.),* the midway-style amusement park has a 1936 Ferris wheel, a carousel, bumper cars and arcade games.

Orange County Museum of Art★

850 San Clemente Dr, Newport Beach. 949-759-1122. www.ocma.net. Open year-round Tue–Sun 11am–5pm. $7.

Formerly called the Newport Harbor Art Museum, OCMA sits on a grassy slope overlooking the water, and complements its large collection of California art with traveling shows from around the world. Opening onto a sculpture garden, the Gypsy Den serves sandwiches and salads that are fresh and cheap.

Balboa Island

www.balboa-island.com.

Approach this quaint island from the mainland, via Jamboree Road, or from the peninsula, via the 50-cent, three-car ferry. Marine Avenue, which locals call Main Street, has lots of cute shops and restaurants. Be sure to sample a frozen banana, an island tradition.

Watts on the Harbor Cruise

949-291-195. www.wattsontheharbor.com

If you really want to get to know the place, reserve a space on a two-hour narrated **harbor cruise.** You'll be wined and dined and regaled with stories by your captain/host as you quietly chug by charming Cape Cod–style cottages, elaborate over-the-top mansions and magnificent yachts.

The venues listed below were selected for their ambience, location and/or value for money. Rates indicate the average cost of an appetizer, an entrée and a dessert for one person (not including tax, gratuity or beverages). Most restaurants are open daily and accept major credit cards. Call for information regarding reservations, dress code and opening hours. For a complete listing of restaurants mentioned in this guide, see Index.

$$$$ over $50	**$$ $15–$30**
$$$ $30–$50	**$ under $15**

Luxury

Bastide $$$$ French

8475 Melrose Pl., Hollywood. Dinner only. Closed Sun & Mon. 323-651-5950.

Chef Alain Giraud delighted diners at Citrus before opening his much-acclaimed restaurant on Melrose, where French designer Andre Putman transformed a Hollywood bungalow into a peaceful dining space with sheer blue window coverings and crystal beaded curtains. Giraud's exquisite Provencal dishes are composed in a selection of impeccably presented tasting menus. The extensive wine list leans heavily on French wines and features some 40 selections by the glass.

Grace $$$$ New American

7360 Beverly Blvd., Hollywood. Dinner only. Closed Mon. 323-934-4400. www.gracerestaurant.net.

In keeping with the restaurant's name, roomy banquettes and white-clothed tables fill Grace's warm, open dining room. Chef Neil Fraser's regularly changing menu marries the freshest seasonal flavors: tenderloin of wild boar with violet-mustard sauce; sautéed Tasmanian steelhead salmon with celery-root velouté; grilled breast of Woodland Farm duck with carrot-ginger emulsion. For dessert, pastry chef Elisabeth Belkind does a mean marzipan-kumquat terrine. Grace's wine list features French burgundies rarely seen on the left coast.

La Cachette $$$$ French

10506 Little Santa Monica Blvd., Century City. 310-470-4992.
www.lacachetterestaurant.com.

Well before it became trendy in the mid-1990s, Jean-Francois Meteigner banked that that Angelenos would appreciate light French food. Luckily, he was right. At La Cachette ("the hideaway" in French) his flair reigns in Provencal-style dishes, such as a rich bouillabaisse of clams, mussels and fish served with spicy rouille; and a cassoulet of duck confit, chicken sausage and braised lamb. Save room for one of the wonderful, warm fruit tarts.

L'Orangerie $$$$ French

903 N. La Cienega Blvd., West Hollywood. Dinner only. Closed Mon. 310-652-9770.
www.orangerie.com.

Dinner at L'Orangerie is what a special-occasion meal should be: warm and welcoming service, carefully prepared fresh ingredients, artful presentation. Of course, all this comes at a pre-mium price, but it's worth the splurge (the signature dish is a silky shirred egg served in the shell and topped with Petrossian sevruga caviar). Jackets are required in L'Orangerie's dining room, which recalls an opulent French chateau.

Mélisse $$$$ French

1104 Wilshire Blvd., Santa Monica. Dinner only. 310-395-0881. www.melisse.com.

This sunny yellow dining room transports patrons to the South of France with hand-painted china, fresh-cut flowers, and original paintings of the French countryside. Chef Josiah Citrin, who founded Jiraffe with Ralph Lunetta, now rules over the kitchen here. His Mediterranean-inspired food takes its cue from the restaurant's name—mélisse is French for lemon balm, an herb native to the Mediterranean. Go during truffle season for the special truffle menu (think fresh tagliatelle with grated black truffles, and truffled rotisserie chicken).

Nobu Malibu
$$$$ Japanese

3835 Cross Creek Rd., in the Malibu Country Mart, Malibu. Dinner only. 310-317-9140. www.nobumatsuhisa.com.

A 1999 addition to sushi wunderkind Nobu Matsuhisa's global network of restaurants, Nobu Malibu brings the chef's exotic ingredients and innovative recipes to the beach. Of course, devotees still flock to Matsuhisa, Nobu's flagship in Beverly Hills. The cozy Malibu destination is favored by celebrities, as well as less famous lovers of incredible sushi. Share the Bento box—a mosaic of green-tea ice cream, a chocolate soufflé and broiled plums with meringue—for dessert

Noé
$$$$ New American

251 S. Olive St., in the Omni Los Angeles Hotel, Downtown. Dinner only. 213-356-4100. www.omnihotels.com/losangelesdining.

English chef Robert Gadsby brings foodies downtown to the Omni Hotel with his surprising New American cuisine. You'll find both Asian and French influences in dishes like gingered butternut squash cappuccino, and baked halibut served with ratatouille and periwinkle chowder. In addition to the a la carte selections, daily chef's tasting menus offer a choice of six ($65) or nine ($95) courses. The California Plaza location, just steps from the Music Center and the new Walt Disney Concert Hall, makes this a good choice for pre- and post-theater dining.

The Palm
$$$$ American

9001 Santa Monica Blvd., West Hollywood. 310-550-8811. www.thepalm.com.

Some things never change, nor should they: a bustling bar, businessmen crowding the booths, colorful caricatures on the wall, brisk competent service from a professional wait staff, and a casual ambience that's as American as apple pie. You'll get expense-account-size portions of steak, grilled lobster, crisp cottage fries, fried onions and New York cheesecake here. This isn't the place to watch your weight!

Patina
$$$$ California-French

141 S. Grand Ave., in the Walt Disney Concert Hall, Downtown. 213-972-3331. www.patinagroup.com.

Only Frank Gehry's dramatic architecture surpasses the delectable dining experience at Patina's new downtown location in the Walt Disney Concert Hall. Award-winning German-born chef Joachim Splichal moved his acclaimed Patina restaurant from its original (1989) location in Hollywood to the new Concert Hall in fall 2003. Here he  continues his tradition of serving creative French-inspired fare, such as sautéed loup de mer with cannelini beans, chorizo sausage and rapini; champagne and Tahitian vanilla-bean risotto with Maine lobster tail; and braised veal cheeks with parsnip purée. Nightly tasting menus are also available.

Saddle Peak Lodge $$$$ American

419 Cold Canyon Rd., Calabasas. Dinner & Sun brunch. 818-222-3888.
www.saddlepeaklodge.com.

Plan the drive to Saddle Peak Lodge for the first time in daylight, so you can appreciate the spectacular scenery in Malibu Canyon. Game is the specialty here: elk tenderloin is roasted and napped with creamy wild mushroom sauce; buffalo is "cooked on the range" with twice-baked potato and creamed spinach; and roasted breast of pheasant is topped with Dijon mustard and bread crumbs. Can't decide on a dessert? Try the sampler—tastes of chocolate-macadamia-nut tart, frozen mascarpone soufflé, chocolate crème brûlée, fresh berries, and warm banana and huckleberry bread pudding. It's perfect for sharing.

Spago Beverly Hills $$$$ California

176 N. Canon Dr., Beverly Hills. 310-385-0880. www.wolfgangpuck.com.

When Wolfgang Puck moved to Beverly Hills from West Hollywood, the cognoscenti followed. Trendy restaurants come and go, but Spago, with its rich mahogany wood, Italian marble and jewel tones, endures as a modern classic. Puck's contemporary dishes speak in French and Asian accents in such dishes as braised lamb daube with parmesan gnocchi, broiled Japanese black cod, and sushi hand roll, but you can also order "Wolfgang's childhood favorites" like Wienerschnitzel. Fortunately, LA's mild climate is conducive to eating in the lovely open-air garden, with its 100-year-old olive trees and granite fountain. *Jacket and tie requested.*

Valentino $$$$ Italian

3115 Pico Blvd., Santa Monica. Closed Sun. 310-829-4313. www.welovewine.com.

Piero Selvaggio created this restaurant for lovers of fine food and wine, who appreciate the seasonally changing menu and the selection of 2,500 bottles in the upstairs wine cellar. Valentino seduces with the finest Italian olive oils, prosciutto from Parma, white truffles from Piedmont and fish flown in fresh from the Adriatic Sea. The chefs will gladly design a menu of small courses around your choice of wine.

Moderate

A.O.C. $$$ Tapas

8022 W. 3rd St., West Hollywood. Dinner only. 323-653-6359. www.aocwinebar.com.

The ladies from Lucques, Suzanne Goin and Caroline Styne, created this wildly popular wine bar and restaurant. Named for the French commission that regulates wine and cheese— *Appellation d'Origine Contrôlée*—A.O.C.'s menu focuses on small plates. Locals nosh on servings of cheeses, house-cured ham and boudin noir, vol au vent brimming with mushrooms, or garlicky manila clams steamed in sherry. Everything, including 50 wines by the glass, is also available at the eight-seat charcuterie bar.

Bistro 45 $$$ French

45 S. Mentor Ave., Pasadena. 626-795-2478. www.bistro45.com.

If you have only one meal in Pasadena, make it at Bistro 45. The staff has been transforming market-fresh ingredients into scrumptious meals for 14 years. Choose ahi tuna crusted with black and white sesame seeds and served with a soy-ginger sauce; grilled Prime dry-aged New York strip with lavender-mustard sauce; pan-roasted Dive boat scallops with plum-tomato and saffron fondue; or roasted breast of Sonoma Range chicken with goat-cheese gnocchi—and be sure to ask owner, Robert Simon, to select the perfect wine pairing.

Café del Rey $$$ Mediterranean

4451 Admiralty Way, Marina del Rey. 310-823-6395. www.tavistockrestaurants.com.

Dine with a view at this bright, airy and contemporary space overlooking the marina. Inside, there's a cozy bar with a fireplace and savory, complex Mediterranean fare such as pistachio-crusted rack of lamb served with pasta and ratatouille, and blackened swordfish with grilled bananas and creamy saffron risotto. The wine list is noteworthy.

Campanile $$$ Mediterranean

624 S La Brea Ave., West Hollywood. 323-938-1447. www.campanilerestaurant.com.

Campanile's soaring two-story space, built by Charlie Chaplin as his office in 1929, boasts a beautiful courtyard enhanced by a fountain, Romanesque arches and brick walls. In 1989 husband-and-wife team Mark Peel and Nancy Silverton founded Campanile and La Brea Bakery here. As executive chef, Mark oversees the food, while Nancy works her magic with pastries and artisan breads—lauded as the best in the city. You can't go wrong with entrées like sautéed Copper River salmon, grilled prime rib with black-olive tapenade, or rosemary-charred baby lamb. For dessert? Perhaps a warm brioche accompanied by apricots, peaches and boysenberries, napped with sabayon.

Cinch $$$ French-Asian

1519 Wilshire Blvd. at 16th St., Santa Monica. Dinner only. 310-395-4139. www.cinchrestaurant.com.

This Santa Monica newcomer features a stunning design highlighted by burled wood, faux-stone walls and mosaic light fixtures. Main courses range from wok-seared New Zealand blue nose grouper to soba noodles with twice-cooked pork; there are vegetarian choices, too. No sweet tooth? End your meal with a selection of cheeses served with pear and quince paste. If you go during mid-week, try the five-course tasting menu *($55)*. Patrons at the bar can order a la carte sushi or light fare along with an extensive list of martinis.

Dan Tana's$$$ Italian

9071 Santa Monica Blvd., West Hollywood. Dinner only. 310-275-9444.

There's nothing sleek about Dan Tana's. Dark paneling, a dimly-lit dining room, Chianti bottles hanging from the ceiling, are all very un-LA. Since 1964, though, Hollywood moguls and mavens—and foodies from out of town—have been squeezing past each other to sit in these red leatherette booths. This isn't fancy food, it's Sunday dinner, the Old World Italian way: spaghetti with Bolognese sauce, chicken parmagiana, veal scallopine and chicken cacciatore.

Geoffrey's$$$ California-Asian

27400 Pacific Coast Hwy., Malibu. 310-457-1519. www.geoffreysmalibu.com.

Locals come to Geoffrey's as much for the food as for the view. Sure, it's a winding drive up PCH (Pacific Coast Highway to the uninitiated) to this hidden aerie, but well worth it. The romantic patio's the place to sit for spectacular Pacific vistas, but wherever you light, you're sure to savor deftly prepared Cal-Asian cuisine—sautéed day boat scallops with Hudson Valley foie gras risotto, coriander-crusted albacore tuna, slow-braised lamb osso buco with creamy polenta. Just sit back, drink in the view and listen to the waterfall splashing in the background.

Jiraffe$$$ French

502 Santa Monica Blvd., Santa Monica. Dinner only. 310-917-6671. www.jirafferestaurant.com.

When "the surfing chef," Ralph Lunetta, isn't trying to catch the perfect wave, you can find him in the kitchen of his Santa Monica bistro, dishing up what he refers to as "sophisticated comfort food." Dinner here could start with purple Peruvian potato gnocchi and Florida rock shrimp, or slow-roasted organic tomato tart. Striped bass comes with peeky toe crab and preserved Meyer lemon spaghettini; dry-aged rib-eye steak is served with potatoes Lyonnaise and creamed spinach. On Monday nights, there's a three-course prix-fixe bistro menu—at $19, it's about half the usual cost of a meal here.

Katana$$$ Japanese

8439 W Sunset Blvd., West Hollywood. Dinner only. 323-650-8585. www.innovativedining.com.

As you enter the dining room at Katana, every chef shouts a greeting in Japanese from the open grill. It's here that the chefs turn out sizzling *robata yaki*, skewers of fish, meat and vegetables, cooked the traditional way, over an open hearth. Located in the first floor of a 1927 office building on a busy section of Sunset, the restaurant incorporates the elements of fire, stone and metal into its edgy design. Things really start hopping about 9:30pm, when the glitterati drop in for a seemingly endless variety of small skewers, from Pacific spiny lobster to chicken meatballs to asparagus wrapped in bacon. These gems from the charcoal grill are each served as they're cooked—this is grazing at its best.

Koi $$$ Japanese

730 N. La Cienega Blvd., West Hollywood. 310-659-9449. www.koirestaurant.com.

Incorporating statuary, horseshoe-shaped booths and a sunken lounge, the design of this West Hollywood eatery adheres to the principles of feng shui, creating a balance of custom-designed furniture, earth tones and soft lighting. Japanese fare bears California touches in such signature dishes as Kobe beef filet mignon, black cod bronzed with miso, and jumbo soft-shell crab. Want something lighter? The menu also features tempura, sushi, sashimi and a variety of rolls. Wash your meal down with a selection from the impressive list of sakes.

Le Dome $$$ California-French

8720 Sunset Blvd., West Hollywood. 310-659-6919.

Elton John was among the founders of this Sunset Strip legend, long the place to "take a lunch" for Tinseltown power brokers. Still a great spot for star-gazing, Le Dome recently reopened after a fire, late in 2003. Designer-of-the-moment Dodd Mitchell's Tuscan-inspired decor added a side entry, an expanded street-front patio and revived the restaurant's famous circular bar. The menu's been updated with the likes of Alaskan halibut and steak tartare, but the caviar and pasta, a classic since 1977, remains.

Lucques $$$ California-French

8474 Melrose Ave., West Hollywood. 323-655-6277. www.lucques.com.

LA native Suzanne Goin's no newcomer to the food scene. Before opening Lucques, she worked in the kitchens of Chez Panisse and Campanile. Fresh seasonal ingredients get a Mediterranean twist here: think Alaskan halibut "bagna cauda" with winter vegetables and pine nuts, or suckling pig with sweet potatoes, romesco sauce, baby spinach and quince. Watching your budget? Go for the three-course prix-fixe dinner on Sunday night; at $35/person, it's one of the best deals in town.

Opaline $$$ Mediterranean

7450 Beverly Blvd., Hollywood. 323-857-6725. www.opalinerestaurant.com.

You might start your meal here with a salad of magenta-fleshed watermelon radish and fennel moistened by champagne vinaigrette, then move on to pan-seared loup de mer with marinated artichokes, or sautéed skatewing accompanied by celery-root purée. Desserts tempt with the likes of Valrhona chocolate torte and pineapple tarte tatin. You can sample small plates and taste any three wines offered by the glass (for $10) next door to the dining room in the Den. Opaline prides itself on serving "honest" wines, that is, ones with unadulterated flavors that aptly represent the region where they are grown.

Table 8 $$$ California

7661 Melrose Ave., Los Angeles. Dinner only. Closed Sun. 323-782-8258. www.table8la.com.

Table 8 opened in late 2003 to rave reviews, both for chef Govind Armstrong's take on regional cuisine and for the restaurant's shimmering and sophisticated interior. Armstrong, whose credits include stints at Spago and Patina, searches out farm fresh, mostly organic ingredients. Consider New Zealand snapper with sautéed nettles, or grilled quail with roasted apples and braised endive. Cheese selections include Point Reyes blue and Humboldt Fog, both from California.

Talésai $$$ Thai

9043 Sunset Blvd., West Hollywood. 310-275-9724. www.talesai.com.

All gleaming glass and polished wood, this modern, art-filled space on trendy Sunset Strip dishes up some of the city's best Thai food. Diners agree that the "heavenly duck," marinated in ginger and soy sauce, steamed and then fried to a crisp, lives up to its name. The signature dish is Hidden Treasures, shrimp, crabmeat and squid cooked in chili-coconut sauce and served in a special dish with impressions for the small morsels, each topped with a tiny metal cap. Now there's a second location, **Talésai Café,** which opened in Beverly Hills *(9198 Olympic Blvd.)* with a less expensive menu.

The Grill on the Alley $$$ American

9560 Dayton Way, Beverly Hills. 310-276-0615. www.thegrill.com.

Modeled after the great grills of New York and San Francisco, Grill on the Alley is the epitome of an expense-account restaurant. During lunch and dinner, movie moguls crowd into the leather-lined booths to drink martinis and hash out business deals. The classic cuisine includes prime rib, New York strip steak, filet mignon, and Dungeness crab cakes, as well as comfort food like meat loaf and chicken pot pie.

The Lobster $$$ Seafood

1602 Ocean Ave., Santa Monica. Closed Mon. 310-458-9294. www.thelobster.com.

Serious seafood and stunning sunsets over the Pacific are the draws at this Santa Monica restaurant, where the signature dish is—you guessed it!—lobster. You can have yours (the Maine or Pacific spiny varieties) steamed, grilled or pan roasted. For those who don't like crustaceans, there's a wide range of fish from Alaskan halibut to king salmon to Chilean sea bass—with a couple of steaks thrown in for good measure. Grab a table on the oceanside deck for the best sunset views.

Budget

Border Grill
$$ Mexican

1445 4th St., Santa Monica. 310-451-1655. www.bordergrill.com.

"Two hot tamales," as they're known on the Food TV network, Mary Sue Milliken and Susan Feniger, redefined Mexican food in America when they opened the Border Grill in 1985. Since then, their authentic renditions of Mexican regional dishes have been bringing droves of diners to the lively Santa Monica outpost. Anchiote-marinated pork slow-roasted in a banana leaf; and sautéed rock shrimp with toasted ancho chilies are just a couple of the draws.

Figtrees Café
$$ International

429 Oceanfront Walk, Venice. 310-392-4937. www.figtreescafe.com.

Open from 9am to 9pm daily, Figtrees has been catering to Venice Beach denizens since 1978. The extensive and eclectic menu offers everything from pastas and potstickers to burritos and burgers (think turkey or spinach-nut). Set right on the beach boardwalk, this is a great place to sip a cappuccino and people-watch.

Luna Park
$$ Mediterranean

672 South La Brea Ave. West Hollywood. 323-934-2110. www.lunaparkla.com.

This LA newbie, with its curtained booths and velvet drapes, offers meals that belie their modest prices (you'll find nothing on the menu for more than $16). For starters, share the goat cheese fondue with grilled bread and sliced apples, and wash it down with one of Luna Park's award-winning mojitos. Entrées include local yellowtail, served with olives, capers and tomatoes; and breaded pork cutlet stuffed with mushrooms and Gruyere. Make your own s'mores for dessert.

Mako
$$ Asian

225 S. Beverly Dr., Beverly Hills. 310-288-8338. www.makorestaurant.com.

Mako Tanaka cut his teeth at Wolfgang Puck's Chinois on Main before he and his wife, Lisa Brady, opened their own restaurant in 2000. The small plates here are "food for sharing" as Tanaka call them. Dig into duck potstickers, crispy quail in tangerine sauce, snow crab tempura, or the Bento box combination, which changes daily. If you still have room, try the yuzu meringue tart with tropical fruit and mango sorbet.

Musso and Frank Grill
$$ American

6667 Hollywood Blvd., Hollywood. Closed Sun & Mon. 323-467-7788.

A Hollywood institution since 1919, Musso and Frank Grill has long been a favorite watering hole for screenwriters (F. Scott Fitzgerald and William Faulkner were once regulars). Tall maroon booths provide privacy while you enjoy no-nonsense dishes like liver and onions, short ribs, and lamb chops.

Pete's Café & Bar $$ American

400 S. Main St., Downtown. 213-617-1000. www.petescafe.com.

Pete's attracts power-lunchers to its upscale space, decorated with mosaic tile floors, dark wood paneling and floor-to-ceiling windows. Comfort food is kicked up a notch here: macaroni and cheese is made with white cheddar, asiago and goat cheese, and you can order a side of blue-cheese fries with your burger. The daily three-course prix-fixe menu is a bargain at $15. Live jazz entertains diners on Friday and Saturday nights; on Sunday night, the cafe comes unplugged with acoustic music.

Alejo's $ Italian

4002 Lincoln Blvd. at Washington Blvd., Marina Del Rey. 310-822-0095.

You wouldn't expect to find good food in this nondescript strip-mall store-front, but Alejo's surprises with their tri-color pizzas and tasty, homestyle Italian dishes. Expect waiting lines, communal seating, big portions and lots of garlic. If the Marina location is too cramped for you, there's a newer version down the street in Westchester. Bring your own beer or wine.

Carney's Restaurant $ American

8351 W Sunset Blvd., West Hollywood. 323-654-8300. www.carneytrain.com.

Burgers and hot dogs are the fare *du jour* at this railroad car cum restaurant, just east of Sunset Strip. Family-owned since 1968, Carney's specializes in hefty half-pound burgers, served with or without chili. Of course, you can get chili on your hot dog, too—or ask for a "New Yorker," with mustard and sauerkraut. In carb-conscious LA, lots of folks order theirs sans bun, wrapped in lettuce or a taco instead.

Highland Grounds $ American

742 N. Highland Ave., Hollywood. 323-466-1507. www.highlandgrounds.com.

Voted best outdoor breakfast spot by *L.A. Weekly*, Highland Grounds' morning fare ranges from huevos rancheros to tofu scramble. Even in chilly weather, locals from nearby Hancock Park and Hollywood enjoy the outdoor patio, warmed by a fire pit. For dinner, choose sandwiches, salads, pizzas or Mexican quesa-dillas and tacos. The music scene's an energetic one here with live performances Tuesday through Sunday night.

Pink's Hot Dogs $ American

709 N. La Brea Ave. at Melrose Ave., Hollywood. 323-931-4223. www.pinkshollywood.com.

Folks drive for hours just to stand in line for a chili dog at this family-owned Hollywood legend. Since 1939 Pink's has been serving up a mean all-beef hot dog topped with mustard and onions. There's even a line at breakfast *(Pink's is open daily 9:30am–2am).*

Must Stay: Los Angeles Area Hotels

The properties listed below were selected for their ambience, location and/or value for money. Prices reflect the average cost for a standard double room for two people (not including applicable city or state taxes). Hotels in Los Angeles constantly offer special discount packages. Price ranges quoted do not reflect the California hotel tax of 14%. For a complete list of hotels mentioned in this guide, see Index.

$$$$$	over $300	$$	$75–$125
$$$$	$200–$300	$	less than $75
$$$	$125–$200		

Luxury

Beverly Hills Hotel $$$$$ 224 rooms

9641 Sunset Blvd., Beverly Hills. 310-276-2251. www.beverlyhillshotel.com.

No matter where you've traveled in the world, it's still a thrill to drive up to the legendary "Pink Palace" on Sunset Boulevard. Spacious, sumptuously de-signed rooms come with extras like walk-in closets, in-room fax machines and free high-speed wireless Internet access. This urban gathering place sits on a twelve-acre estate surrounded by lovely gardens, which are the setting for its 21 splendid bungalow suites. A longtime favorite among dealmakers and celeb-rities, the **Polo Lounge ($$$$)** features a jazz brunch on Sundays.

Casa del Mar $$$$$ 129 rooms

1910 Ocean Front Walk, Santa Monica. 310-581-5533 or 800-898-6999. www.hotelcasadelmar.com.

When you enter the Casa del Mar, be prepared to step back in time to the lavish lifestyle of the roaring twenties, when Santa Monica knew its heyday. Built in 1929, the Casa del Mar Beach Club was refurbished to its previous opu-lence in 1999 with high-tech amenities and a business center for traveling CEOs. Guest rooms sport a beach motif, with gauzy drapes, floor-to-ceiling windows and soft pastel hues. Add to that breathtaking ocean views (but no balconies), a Mediterranean-style pool and gardens, and a fitness room and spa.

Four Seasons Hotel Los Angeles at Beverly Hills $$$$$ 285 rooms

300 S. Doheny Dr. 310-273-2222 or 800-819-5053. www.fourseasons.com.

Warm, personalized service is the Four Seasons' signature, and this property is no exception. Located in a residential neighborhood adjacent to Beverly Hills and West Hollywood, the hotel offers complementary limousine service within a 2mi radius. Sophisticated public spaces are done in light woods and enhanced by fine artwork. The half-acre pool deck boasts a cafe, a fitness center and whirlpool, all just steps from the full-service spa *(see Must Be Pampered)*. **Gardens ($$$$)** dining room showcases Asian-accented cuisine.

Hotel Bel-Air $$$$$ 90 rooms

701 Stone Canyon Rd., West Los Angeles. 310-472-1211. www.hotelbelair.com.

Tucked away in the canyons above Sunset Boulevard, this complex of pink Mission-style buildings oozes exclusivity. Soon after it opened in 1946, the Bel-Air quickly established a devoted following among Hollywood stars, who were drawn to its casual comfort, privacy and fine service. All of the rooms and suites were recently redecorated with custom fabrics and French country furnishings. Don't miss a walk through the 11 acres of lush **gardens**★★, landscaped with sycamores, live oaks, palms, fig trees and bright flowers.

Raffles L'Ermitage $$$$$ 123 rooms

9291 Burton Way, Beverly Hills. 310-278-3344 or 800-800-2113. www.lermitagehotel.com.

Clean lines, light woods and pale colors combine here to create a serene ambience. The hotel's Asian flair is evident in the 12C silk-brocade Chinese textiles that adorn the lobby. In the large rooms, you'll find silk shams, light cotton robes, and handmade sliding wood screens that tastefully hide TVs. Take a dip in the rooftop pool; pump some iron in the fitness room; treat yourself to a massage at the hotel's Amrita Spa, or join local moguls at **Jaan ($$$$)** for creative California cuisine.

Shutters on the Beach $$$$$ 198 rooms

One Pico Blvd., Santa Monica. 310-458-0030 or 800-334-9000. www.shuttersonthebeach.com.

Staying here is like having a luxurious beach house in the city. But the beach-cottage feel belies the stylish service behind the white-shuttered windows at this property—one of only four hotels in LA County that is directly on the beach. Set on the sands near Santa Monica's historic pier, the Cape Cod-style hotel offers balconies or patios facing the ocean, bright white walls and a palette of soft colors inspired by the sea just outside. Sunbathe on the beach, take a soak in your Jacuzzi tub or chill out by the pool—after all, you're on vacation.

The Peninsula $$$$$ 196 rooms

9882 Little Santa Monica Blvd., Beverly Hills. 310-551-2888 or 800-462-7899. www.peninsula.com.

Set in the heart of Beverly Hills, the Peninsula is within easy walking distance of chic Rodeo Drive—but if you don't feel like hoofing it, you can take the hotel's limousine. Rooms are decked out with fine antiques, original artwork and marble baths, in keeping with the luxe neighborhood; 16 private villas stud the landscaped grounds. Check out the lovely rooftop garden, the location of the spa *(see Must Be Pampered)*, cafe and a 60ft lap pool. One of the top-rated restaurants in town, **The Belvedere ($$$$)** features California-French fare.

The Regent Beverly Wilshire $$$$$ 395 rooms

9500 Wilshire Blvd., Beverly Hills. 310-275-5200 or 800-545-4000. www.regenthotels.com/beverlywilshire.

Grande dame of elegance, the Regent Beverly Wilshire sits at Beverly Hills most famous address—where Wilshire Boulevard meets Rodeo Drive. The hotel has long welcomed heads of state, royalty and distinguished guests. Rooms in the Italian Renaissance Wilshire Wing remain true to the hotel's past; while quarters in the Beverly Wing (facing the pool and spa) are coolly contemporary. California cuisine with an Italian accent delights diners in the elegant **Dining Room ($$$$;** jackets recommended), which features live jazz on weekends.

The St. Regis Los Angeles $$$$$ 297 rooms

2055 Avenue of the Stars, Century City. 310-277-6111 or 877-787-3452. www.starwood.com.

The transformation of the high-rise Century Plaza Towers into the St. Regis (part of the Starwood chain's Luxury Collection) is apparent in the upgrades to the quality of its woodwork, furnishings and bathroom fixtures (with a fantastically strong shower). Conveniently located in Century City, just minutes from Beverly Hills, the property offers oversize rooms, sunset views, wireless Internet access, and complimentary newspapers and shoe shines. The intimate St. Regis Spa *(see Must Be Pampered)* is conveniently located next to the fitness center and pool.

Avalon Hotel $$$$ 88 rooms

9400 W. Olympic Blvd., Beverly Hills. 310-277-5221 or 800-535-4715. www.korhotels.com.

Think Isamu Noguchi tables, Charles Eames chairs and George Nelson lamps and you've got the retro vibe at the Avalon. The three-building complex enjoys a good location in a residential neighborhood, just footsteps from Beverly Drive. **Blue on Blue** restaurant (**$$$**) appeals to sophisticates who sip and sup by candlelight on the curved pool terrace or in private cabanas. The restaurant's New American cuisine incorporates fresh ingredients from local farmers' markets.

Loews Santa Monica Beach Hotel $$$$ 342 rooms

1700 Ocean Ave., Santa Monica. 310-458-6700 or 800-235-6397. www.loewshotels.com.

It's always spring in Loews Santa Monica's four-story atrium with its towering palm trees and views of the sea. The hotel boasts direct beach access and lies within walking distance of the Santa Monica Pier and Third Street Promenade. All the guest rooms have recently been redecorated, with chic contemporary decor, and the cable TV offers 60 channels and built-in Internet access—if you can tear yourself away from the ocean views out your window. Relax at the excellent spa, then savor California classics at **Papillon** (**$$$**).

Ritz-Carlton Huntington Hotel & Spa $$$$ 392 rooms

1401 S. Oak Knoll Ave., Pasadena. 626-568-3900 or 800-241-3333. www.ritzcarlton.com.

Nestled in the foothills of the San Gabriel mountains, the Ritz Huntington Hotel has been a Pasadena landmark since 1907. Choose accommodations in the main hotel, or in three separate residential-style buildings. Whichever you choose, you'll enjoy the essence of the California good life, surrounded by mountains and lush gardens, and conveniently located near all the fine attractions Pasadena has to offer. Oh, and don't forget the full-service spa and fitness center.

Ritz-Carlton Marina del Rey $$$$ 304 rooms

4375 Admiralty Way, Marina del Rey. 310-823-1700. www.ritzcarlton.com.

The Ritz Carlton's splendid location on the marina, just 5mi from Los Angeles International Airport makes it a great find for travelers. All the tastefully decorated rooms—what else would you expect from the Ritz?—have marble baths and small private balconies with city or marina views. At **Jer-ne** (**$$$$**), chef Troy Thompson has gained recognition for his fusion fare. Try the foie gras and duck breast served on a rock heated at 500°F for eight hours. Dining alone? Make a friend at the onyx communal table.

Sunset Marquis Hotel & Villas $$$$ 124 rooms

1200 N. Alta Loma Rd., West Hollywood. 310-657-1333 or 800-858-9758.
www.sunsetmarquishotel.com.

Musicians flock to this trendy retreat, just south of Sunset in the hub of the
West Hollywood scene, where they have access to a state-of-the-art recording
studio. Accommodations range from roomy junior suites to capacious two-
bedroom villas; the latter are favored by celebs who can access them—sans
paparazzi—via the underground garage. Those not wanting to stay hidden can
take a copy of the hotel's guide to "Attention-Deficit Sightseeing" to hunt for
local hotspots. But with the **Whiskey Bar** *(see Nightlife)* right on the premises,
you'll have all the nightlife you want without ever leaving the hotel.

Moderate

Ambrose $$$ 77 rooms

1255 20th St. at Arizona St., Santa Monica. 310-315-1555. www.ambrosehotel.com.

Wellness is the focus of Santa Monica's newest
boutique hotel, opened in spring 2003. An Asian-
inspired ambience pervades the property, which
encompasses a serene garden and koi pond.
Rooms have high ceilings, hardwood floors, Italian
linens and Aveda toiletries. Fitted with everything
from a ballet bar to yoga videos (yes, they have
the standard fitness equipment, too), the Rec Room encourages guests to keep
up their healthy lifestyle. Breakfast is included in the rate, and **Drago** restaurant provides 24-hour room service from its all-organic menu.

The Beverly Hilton $$$ 579 rooms

9876 Wilshire Blvd., Beverly Hills. 310-274-7777 or 800-445-8667. www.hilton.com.

Backdrop for the Golden Globes, the American Film Institute dinner, and many
other celebrity events, this hotel is just a short walk from Rodeo Drive. Rooms
are done in cherry woods, and come equipped with fluffy robes. A fitness
center, an Olympic-size pool, and complementary limousine service within a
3mi radius round out the amenities. **Trader Vics ($$$$)**, the famed Polynesian-
style restaurant and lounge, is a popular late-night rendezvous.

Georgian Hotel $$$ 56 rooms

1415 Ocean Ave., Santa Monica. 310-395-9945 or 800-538-8147. www.georgianhotel.com.

Step back to the early days of LA's film industry at this turquoise and gold Art Deco gem across the street from Santa
Monica beach. The lobby is decorated true to the early 1930s
with geometric marble floors and a pink, green and black
color scheme. Rooms received a $2 million facelift in 2000;
all offer either city or ocean views. Rates include continental
breakfast served on the veranda in the morning, and wine in
the afternoon; small pets are welcome.

Le Merigot $$$ 175 rooms

1740 Ocean Ave., Santa Monica. 310-395-9700 or 888-539-7899. www.lemerigothotel.com.

This J.W. Marriott beach hotel and spa *(see Must Be Pampered)* faces the palm-lined Pacific just a short walk from Santa Monica Pier, Palisades Park and the Third Street Promenade. France's Cote d'Azur provided the inspiration for Le Merigot's sunny European elegance, which the property tempers with California-casual style. Pillowtop beds, Frette linens, down duvets and feather pillows assure a good night's sleep. At **Cézanne ($$$)** you can sample classic French fare from Dover sole meunière to veal medallions forestière.

Le Montrose Suite Hotel $$$ 133 rooms

900 Hammond St., West Hollywood. 310-855-1115 or 800-776-0666. www.lemontrose.com.

An all-suite Art Deco-style hotel, Le Montrose is located in a quiet, residential neighborhood within walking distance of Sunset Strip. Ask for one of the 51 newly renovated suites; each one has a refrigerator, a balcony and a fireplace (children under 14 can share the suite free if they don't require extra beds). Bring your racket and try out the lighted rooftop tennis court—there's a pool up there, too.

Loews Beverly Hills Hotel $$$ 137 rooms

1224 S. Beverwil Dr., Beverly Hills. 310-277-2800 or 800-235-6397. www.loewshotels.com.

This sunlit 137-room boutique hotel, just footsteps from where Rodeo Drive starts winding north through Beverly Hills, offers a great location plus person-alized service. Rooms are done in black and tan or peach and cream, and come with private balconies; some rooms have whirlpool tubs. The poolside dining room, **Lot 1224 ($$$)**, and adjacent lounge—complete with pool table—are favorite gathering spots. At the restaurant, chef Eric Rillos deftly prepares hearty American fare with Asian and Mediterranean flair; his popcorn shrimp is a must-try!

Luxe Hotel Rodeo Drive $$$ 92 rooms

360 N. Rodeo Dr., Beverly Hills. 310-273-0300 or 800-468-3541. www.luxehotels.com.

Leave the car behind. All the boutiques of Rodeo Drive lie literally at your doorstep at the Luxe—and the hotel's rates won't break the bank (unlike some of the nearby shops!). Sleek is the name of the decor here, which manages to be minimalist without being cold. There's even a pool on the second floor.

Millennium Biltmore Hotel $$$ 683 rooms

506 S. Grand Ave. (between 5th & 6th Sts.), Downtown. 213-624-1011 or 800-245-8673.
www.millenniumhotels.com.

Visiting a historic landmark is one thing, but staying in one is an extra-special treat. In this Italianate-style hotel, built in 1923, you can swim in the lavishly tiled indoor pool, have high tea in historic **Rendezvous Court** *(see Landmarks)* and stroll corridors where royalty, presidents and celebrities have all walked before you (the Biltmore has served as the set of many a film and TV show). Rooms are decorated with French provincial furnishings and soothing neutral tones. The hotel's location (across the street from the Pershing Square metro stop) provides easy access to downtown attractions, including the new Walt Disney Concert Hall, four blocks away.

Park Hyatt Los Angeles $$$ 366 rooms

2151 Avenue of the Stars, Century City. 310-277-1234 or 800-778-7477.
www.parklosangeles.hyatt.com.

You'll love how this hotel looks and feels after its recent $14 million renovation. The lobby, with its marble floor and glass-enclosed atrium, is an inviting place to unwind and listen to live piano music. Sunny yellow rooms (more than half are suites) claim balconies with great views, 300-thread-count Italian sheets, and oversize marble bathrooms with separate showers and tubs. Mineral water, a shoe shine, the daily newspaper, and limo service to nearby Beverly Hills are all complementary.

Venice Beach House Historic Inn $$$ 9 rooms

15 30th Ave., Venice. 310-823-1966. www.venicebeachhouse.com.

It's rare to find a B&B that's listed on the National Historic Registry, but this one is. Built in 1911, the ivy-covered residence is set in a large-for-Venice landscaped garden just steps from the beach. Individually decorated rooms have both floral prints and charm, along with such amenities as cable televisions and high-speed Internet access. Plan for buffet breakfasts, drinks in the courtyard and walks to Venice Pier.

Interconnecting?

Budget

Casa Malibu Inn On The Beach $$ 21 rooms

22752 Pacific Coast Hwy., Malibu. 310-456-2219 or 800-831-0858. www.casamalibu.com.

What a romantic find! You can fall asleep to the rhythmic sound of the waves at this little beachfront B&B. Rooms have soaring wood ceilings and private decks; most feature fireplaces, and some suites have kitchenettes. There's even a flower-filled patio for relaxing. Enjoy a complementary continental breakfast with fresh-baked pastries from Wolfgang Puck's local restaurant. Casa Malibu doesn't have a pool, but who needs one when the ocean is nearly at your doorstep?

Farmer's Daughter Hotel
$$ 66 rooms

115 S. Fairfax St., West Hollywood. 323-937-3930 or 800-334-1658. www.farmersdaughterhotel.com.

Farmer's Daughter, recognizable by its blue-gingham painted exterior, faces the Farmers Market and the Grove outdoor mall. Managing partners Peter and Ellen Picataggio opened the property in November 2003, with its funky barnyard theme: hand-stitched denim bedspreads, lattice head-boards, whitewashed floors, rooster-print wallpaper, cow-skin rugs, milk-pail accessories and a gingham-clad staff. This budget hotel raises the bar with concierge service, free high-speed Internet access and in-room DVDs.

Hotel del Flores
$$ 40 rooms

409 N. Crescent Dr., Beverly Hills. 310-274-5115.

This intimate, two-story inn lies within walking distance of the attractions in the Beverly Hills triangle. The 40 small rooms are clean and quiet. Some have queen beds; some have private baths. Count on just the basic television here—no cable, no Internet access.

Saga Motor Hotel
$$ 70 rooms

1633 E. Colorado Blvd., Pasadena. 626-795-0431 or 800-793-7242. www.thesagamotorhotel.com.

If you're in town on New Year's Day (when the otherwise-reasonable rates soar), this family-owned and operated motel makes a great vantage point for watching the Rose Bowl Parade, which passes right out front. Its recently renovated rooms form a U shape around a flower bedecked pool.

Sportsmen's Lodge Hotel
$$ 191 rooms

12825 Ventura Blvd. at Coldwater Canyon, Studio City. 818-769-4700. www.slhotel.com.

A San Fernando Valley destination that charged $9 a room when Clark Gable frequented the place, this hotel is still a good bargain. Its newly renovated rooms with king beds and high-speed Internet access are priced at $15 over the hotel's $124 standard rate. Grab a bite at the old-fashioned Patio Cafe and adjacent Caribou restaurant or have a drink at the Muddy Moose Bar. Besides an Olympic-size pool and Jacuzzi, the hotel offers complementary transporta-tion to Universal Studios—not to mention discount tickets for the Universal Studios Tour *(see Studios).*

The Standard Downtown
$$ 207 rooms

550 South Flower St., Downtown. 213-892-8080. www.standardhotel.com.

Even more stunning than its West Hollywood sibling, the Standard Downtown opened about a year and half ago. The decor is ultra contemporary and corporate-chic with an eye to comfort: big beds, complementary high-speed Internet access and tubs for two. For exer-cise, there's a fitness club (open 24/7) and a rooftop pool, with fantastic views of the downtown skyline.

Index

Index

Photo Credits

YOUR OPINION MATTERS!

Thank you for purchasing a Michelin Travel Publications product. To help us continue to offer you the absolute best in travel guides, maps and atlases, we need your feedback.

Please fill in this questionnaire and return it to:

Michelin Travel Publications – Attn: Marketing
P.O. Box 19001
Greenville, SC 29602-9001, USA

To thank you, we will draw one name from the returned questionnaires each month from May 2004 to year end. Each month's winner will receive a free 2004 North America Road Atlas, or a set of the Must SEES travel guides, or a set of the Regional Road Atlas + Travel Guides.

1. How would you rate the following features of the product, if applicable?

1 = Very Good   2 = Acceptable   3 = Poor

	1	2	3
Selection of attractions/sights	☐	☐	☐
Practical information (prices, etc.)	☐	☐	☐
Description of establishments	☐	☐	☐
General presentation	☐	☐	☐
Cover	☐	☐	☐

2. How satisfied were you with this product?

☐ Very satisfied   ☐ Satisfied   ☐ Somewhat Satisfied   ☐ Not Satisfied

If not satisfied, how should we improve the product? _____

3. Did you buy this product: (check all that apply)

☐ For holiday/vacation
☐ For short breaks or weekends
☐ For business purposes
☐ As a gift
☐ Other

4. Where would you buy and expect our products to be available? (check all that apply)

☐ Supermarket   ☐ Mass Merchandiser (Costco, Sam's, etc.)
☐ Convenience store   ☐ Specialty store (museum shop, travel store, etc.)
☐ Bookstore   ☐ Gas/Service Station
☐ Online   ☐ Kiosk/Gift shop

5. Which destinations do you visit the most often for pleasure? (list as many locations as you wish) _____

Tear Here

Tear Here

6. Which destinations do you visit the most often for business? (list as many locations as you wish)

_____

7. When you go on vacation, generally how long do you stay?
(check all that apply)
- ☐ Three or four days
- ☐ One week
- ☐ Two weeks
- ☐ A combination of short (three or four days) and one-week vacations
- ☐ Other

8. When you travel, what mode of transportation do you most frequently use?
(1 - most frequent, 6 - least frequent)

Plane _____ Car _____ Bus _____ Train _____ Cruise _____ Other _____

9. Would you consider buying other Michelin travel books or products?
- ☐ Yes   ☐ No
If yes, which one(s):
- ☐ Must SEES
- ☐ North America 2004 Road Atlas
- ☐ North America Regional Road Atlas + Travel Guide
- ☐ North America Regional Road Atlas
- ☐ North America Regional Maps
- ☐ Green Guide (North American titles)
- ☐ Green Guide (European titles)
- ☐ Red Guide
- ☐ European City Maps
- ☐ Other

10. Your age?
- ☐ Less than 25 years old
- ☐ 25–35 years old
- ☐ 36–45 years old
- ☐ 46–55 years old
- ☐ 56–65 years old
- ☐ 65 years plus

11. Additional Comments:

Telephone or e-mail where we may reach you:

_____

If you would like to be added to our mailing list, please fill out the information below:

☐ Ms.   ☐ Mrs.   ☐ Mr.

Name _____

Address _____

City _____ State _____

Zip Code _____ Country _____

E-mail (optional): _____